HAVE IT ALL

KRIS KROHN

HAVE

IT

ALL

The Roadmap to Becoming a
SELF-MADE MILLIONAIRE

For more information contact:
1440 Moon River Dr.
Provo, UT 84604
email: support@kriskrohn.com
phone: 801-691-0375

KRISKROHN.COM

Instagram: @kriskrohn
Facebook: @MentorwithKris
YouTube Channel: Kris Krohn
Podcast: Have It All
TikTok: @kriskrohn
Twitter: @kriskrohnREI
LinkedIn: @MentorwithKris

ISBN (softcover): 978-1-7379209-0-8

First Edition

The Library of Congress Cataloging-in-Publication data on file

Writer and Project Manager: Jennifer Lill Brown
Cover and Interior Designer: Marisa Jackson

DEDICATION

To all of the individuals who should have been educated about money but weren't. The information in this book should have been given to you in high school or college, but it wasn't. The good news is it's never too late!

This book is the financial foundation that you need to have it all. It is destined to become the new gold standard for financial and wealth education—the foundation upon which all financial success is built.

For everyone determined to have it all, you've got this one life to live. I want you to make the most of it in every possible way.

ACKNOWLEDGMENTS

SOCIETY DOES NOT CURRENTLY FURNISH US with a sufficient level of financial education. This means that my acknowledgments are not dedicated to anyone from my formal years of schooling.

Instead, my acknowledgments belong to dozens of wealthy individuals whose books I've read, courses I've taken, or events I've attended. I'm talking about the most successful people in the world—people that I worked hard and invested time and money to get into proximity and mentor directly with them.

There are more names to mention than I possibly could fit into a few pages. However, I want to take an opportunity to express profound gratitude to a handful of individuals that made the most remarkable contributions to what has become my complete financial freedom roadmap laid out in this book:

To Dolf de Roos, who was once one of Robert Kiyosaki's financial advisors. He is someone who has become a friend, an investment partner, a business partner, and an instrumental part of my journey in so many ways. His first book, *Real Estate Riches*, planted the seed that helped me fully catch the "real estate bug."

To Robert G. Allen, who in time became one of my key business partners. I'm grateful for his books on creative, no-money-down real estate.

To Tony Robbins, who got me out of my funk many times and helped me learn the dynamics of a successful business.

To Roland Frasier, who has had over 100 successful exits and is now my business partner. He taught me the power of building value in the world that can be captured through selling a business for a lot of money.

To Kevin Harrington, who was one of the original sharks on ABC's *Shark Tank*. His influence taught me the power of scaling a business, franchising it, and selling it.

To Garrett White, who inspired me to own my personal power so that I could show up at home and in business.

To Sean Callagy, who has been an incredible mentor and master of the universe when it comes to a genuine, authentic influence.

To Rob Gill, who taught me the most intelligent way to stash cash for my investments.

To Keith Cunningham and Tim Weeks, who taught me how to fully understand accounting and financials to maximize my margins while creating even more value for my customers.

To Carson Tietjen, who is my CEO and who kindly pushed me out of the way so he could lead and build an empire so much bigger, stronger, and more inspired than I ever could have.

To Chris Milliner, who is my Director of Operations. He reminded me to always watch my six, protect what we've grown, and be faithful to the mission.

To Tyler Bennett, who helped me build the systems to transact thousands of properties, completely turn-key.

To Marianne Hickman, who is my sales floor manager and masterful breakthrough artist. She has been with me every step of the journey to empower people and help them crush their limiting beliefs.

To my wife, Kalenn Krohn, and our children, who remain my central motivation for how I spend my time.

Finally, I give the ultimate credit to God for countless revelations that led to my purpose and understanding of how to build wealth so I could then share it with the world.

TABLE OF CONTENTS

PART ONE

EXPOSING SOCIETY'S BROKEN PLAN

All human societies
go through fads in
which they temporarily
either adopt practices of
little use or else
abandon practices of
considerable use.

JARED DIAMOND

JUST ANOTHER GIMMICK?

MOST THINGS IN LIFE come and go.

Who won the Superbowl in 2001? Chances are you don't have a clue. What did you have for dinner this time seven months ago? It'd be a little weird if you knew. Remember that day you spilled ketchup on your shirt in middle school? Probably not.

However, a few things seem to affect *everything*, whether we want them to or not—and money is the most obvious one.

While money should never be the sole focus of your existence, let's face it: Money dictates so much. From the car you drive, your home, and your neighborhood to the schools your kids have access to, the vacations you take, and the donations you give to others, money rules.

With money, the sky's the limit. Without money, there's pretty much nothing but limits.

So, let's get one thing straight. If you are looking for an emotional healing book, this isn't it. I highly recommend you study a balanced range of topics, and emotional health is as much a part of having it all as is financial health. But right here and right now?

This is a book about money.

Even more than that, it's about how to outsmart *old money* rules and follow *new* ones that grow your net worth to new, unfathomable heights. Money is a game, and every game has rules. If you learn the rules, you win; and if you don't? You can figure that one out.

Tragically, society is a terrible money coach. Like, the *worst*. Society teaches us to want flashy cars and big houses, but it doesn't tell us how to actually acquire them. College doesn't have any "Rules of Money" course that I ever saw. And financial planners? They pretend they have all the answers, but, like every other industry, the financial world's genuine experts are few and far between.

If you've been following society's established money rules until now, you have learned how to place that money into the hands of "experts" to yield insufficient, single-digit returns. At some point, it may have dawned on you that, with your current returns, retirement is looking a little more terrifying with each passing year.

Are you going to outlive your money?

The odds are stacked against you—if you continue to play by old rules.

The Only Constant is Change

The good news is that if you put five specific investments to work for you, you will create the kind of wealth you thought only the "lucky" few ever make. We will be discussing some sizeable returns—but why would you read a book about money that didn't promise a healthy return on investment (ROI) on your time? I have *no idea* why anyone would read a book about money that does not promise to deliver a plan to build massive wealth.

Would you buy a book that promises, "Read this, and you might make more money at some point?" I hope not.

So, why another book about money? Hasn't it all been said?

I've observed this attitude a lot over the years—about everything. Since I was a kid, people have said things like, "It's all been said," or "There is nothing new under the sun."

For the sake of argument, let's assume that is true.

Before the Internet, the world thought that business would always be conducted in person. That changed, didn't it? Before social media, the world believed that the only way to advertise was TV, email, newspaper, and billboards. Now, the only advertising with decent returns is done through social media.

There are other examples—the changes in how we buy, how we network, how we teach, how we practice medicine, how we travel, how we eat, and much more. I laugh when I think about how I used to invest in real estate by driving around neighborhoods all day long and meeting with realtors. Now I make more than ever, all from my couch.

Let's face it: The only thing we can count on is that *everything* changes.

That means you have a choice. You either use the new rules and stay up to speed, or you use the old rules and get left behind.

When it comes to money, getting "left behind" means you use broken, outdated investment rules that force you to live with a scarcity mentality. You forge ahead toward your retirement years, devoid of any confidence that you'll have enough money to enjoy life after the daily grind.

Let's say you trusted the commonly held beliefs about wealth accumulation and did what you were told by financial advisors for years. You then realize decades later that you have to live on only 10 to 20 percent of your pre-retirement income, or else you'll run out of money.

I can't speak for you, but c'mon. Wouldn't that make you feel hoodwinked? Well, it happens to people every single day in this country—to people who are using the old rules. That is why I say that everything you need to know about money has *not* been written and will never be written.

The way we earn and spend money in the present constantly changes so the way we invest that money for the future should change as well.

I'm dumbfounded at the financial plans that the industry considers to be sound advice—from 401(k)s and IRAs to "balanced" stock portfolios filled with nothing but blue-chip stocks. Experts also claim that paying off your mortgage is a sound investment. All of this planning and saving is for single-digit returns at best!

You deserve better.

You deserve to know that as long as you put your money into an investment that produces single-digit returns, you will only have a small fraction of what you hoped to one day call your nest egg.

The Storm That Revealed My Purpose

I have spoken with many highly successful people over the years. Each of their stories seems to have one fascinating thing in common. During their lives, there was a point at which they felt they were going through the motions.

Have you ever felt that way? Like you're on autopilot? That mode of operation tends to make you feel emotionally devoid. It could also make your life feel a little light on meaning.

Until one day, when you experience "the moment" that sparks your awakening. You suddenly realize you have choices—and you recognize you've been making the wrong ones. You finally understand this is *your* life and your one shot.

My awakening came after I nearly died.

I had just graduated high school. My five younger siblings and I were on vacation with our parents, the last holiday I would have before I left to serve a two-year church mission. We were enjoying some lazy days in Cannon Beach, Oregon, just outside of Portland. It's a quaint little town—a sleepy place to get away from everything.

One afternoon, my sister and I decided to go wave jumping. The water was unusually shallow in one area of the beach. We traveled about a tenth of a mile out from the shoreline, and the water was still only waist high. Looking back toward shore, the rest of our family were tiny specks on the beach.

My sister must have been feeling brave or reckless because she continued walking further and further out. The blustery day had produced frigid, bone-chilling water temperatures—and with the freezing temperatures came a sudden tempest. We began rolling in waves that were rising what felt like 10 feet high. One colossal wave lifted me up into the sky, pushing me further out to sea.

Still, we pressed on. Ah, the stupidity of youth.

Suddenly, as a wave I was riding crashed down, I could no longer find my footing. I instantly knew we had pushed Mother Nature to her limits, and she was now going to put us back in check.

A riptide pulled my feet right out from under me and sucked me deeper into the ocean.

I quickly started swimming back, but I looked in horror when I could stand up again as I saw my sister being carried out even further by the waves. I could tell from the terror in her eyes that she knew she was in imminent danger. But she was already fatigued, and her strength was quickly fading.

I panicked and turned toward the shore to ride the next wave as high as possible into the sky. As I reached the peak, I thrust my body up and flailed my arms in an attempt to signal danger to my family (who looked like ants at this point). Somehow, I could tell my dad saw me, and he appeared to be running to get help.

Once again, to my horror, by the time I turned around, my sister had been pulled even further away.

I knew in my heart that my dad would not be able to get help in time. To make matters more dire, my lifeguard training told me not to attempt a solo rescue in these conditions. If I tried, there was little chance either of us would survive.

However, I also knew that I would never be able to live with myself if I watched my sister drown. There was only one decision to make—I dove in after her. At first, a sense of heroism washed over me as I swam quickly out to her, and that gave me superhuman (albeit momentary) strength. As I reached her, I could see how tired she was.

Still, I thought, *"I'm going to save my sister."*

I was utterly unprepared for how difficult it would be to keep her head above water as I attempted to swim for both of us. Panic set in yet again, and all of that heroic strength faded. Swimming turned into barely treading water, and both of us were being swept further out to sea again.

The moment finally came when I stopped trying to make it back to shore. Hopelessness washed over me. I was moments away from watching my sister drown, and then I would be next.

That's when it happened.

My life flashed before my eyes, and it was a more painful experience than I thought it would be at the tender age of 19. My thoughts immediately drifted to everything of which I felt ashamed:

I haven't given anything. I haven't created anything. I've only been a drain on others.

I knew there was only one more thing I could do. I shouted to God.

"Save me!"

I'm here to tell you that miracles are real. At that moment, a massive, non-breaking wave carried my sister and me back in the direction of the shore—and back to where the water was waist-high again.

As our feet felt the softness of the sand, we knew we were saved. I should have been dead, but instead, I was alive. As I walked my shaken sister toward the shore, I couldn't stop thinking:

Why did God save me? Why me?

Since that day in those frigid, turbulent waters, I've never taken life for granted. I've pursued life with fiery passion. I've lived in pursuit of *having it all* since the moment I emerged—alive, breathing—out of the ocean.

That moment has led me on a journey of self-discovery, mentorship, learning, and growing. There are so many times it would have been effortless to settle back into mediocrity or take it easy—to take my foot off the gas and enjoy life. But I can't let myself do that.

I have to find and test every limit.

I have to find out how to explore every possibility.

Why Have It All?

Over the years, the mentality that began forming that day in the water has materialized into something that I can teach to others. That is why I built this book upon my "Have It All" philosophy that I've worked to exemplify since that day with my sister. I was saved for a reason, and I believe part of that reason is to teach as many people as possible to have it all.

HAVE IT ALL (VERB):
Striving to live a life worth pursuing by pushing yourself to steadily and endlessly grow in three areas: *health*, *relationships*, and *finances*.

This philosophy has been the driving force in my life, and it all started with that one moment at sea.

When I think of what it means to have it all, it does not mean possessing earthly riches, majestic mansions, or incredible cars. Earthly possessions can be gone in the blink of an eye.

Having it all encompasses the privilege of being on a journey of personal growth and achievement.

For me, that journey often manifests in the form of physical results. Having it all is a health, wealth, and relationship matter, which means I pursue the most enriching relationships. It means that I endeavor to build and maintain the healthiest body possible.

It also means that I consistently transform *money* into *meaning.*

Money is merely a tool that opens the door to possibility. The better you are at making money, the more opportunities you will have to create a more meaningful life.

The Internet is literally overflowing with books and resources that can transform the health of your relationships and help you grow spiritually, mentally, and physically. Where the advice falls short is in the area of financial health.

For some reason, we have yet to see a massive disruption in the financial education space. *Why is that?* I'm not sure, but it may have something to do with the fact that there is so much fear of the unknown regarding the way investments really work.

Instead of learning how money really works, people choose to put blind faith in a person with a few acronyms in their title.

Dave Ramsey is currently the closest thing the sector has to a recognized expert in finance. His message is targeted at those who can't control their spending and need to get out of debt. That's important! But getting out of debt and then investing that money into single-digit return investment vehicles is not enough for those of us who aspire to have it all.

If you want to get out of debt, then get out of debt. This is not a debt solutions book (although I could easily argue that you can get out of debt much faster by increasing your return on investments). At its core, this book is about transforming money into *infinitely more wealth* that will give you the security, peace, and freedom you want and help establish a lasting legacy.

Now, I don't believe in get-rich-quick schemes. I also know that significant results always require action and implementation to attain. What you have to remember is that most of the skeptics in the world don't *implement*. People talk a good game, but precious few commit to the follow-through.

Is it laziness? Fear? Limited mindset?

That's a discussion for another book, perhaps.

If you are a doer and an implementer, you will absolutely thrive by following the new investing rules laid out in this book.

I'm going to be talking about money, and I freely admit that my views are polarizing (the transformational stuff always is). You'll discover that I'm highly opposed to the universally accepted, traditional investment models. I will show you how society's accepted game plan for wealth accumulation is not only flawed—it's utterly broken.

In other words, you stick with the old model, and you're guaranteed to lose. Traditional financial advisors are playing according to old rules. The excellent news is I have the scoop on the new rules—the ones that enable you to actually win.

Do you want to win? Of course, you do! Who doesn't want to win?

Ultimately, my "superpower" is teaching people how to be resourceful.

Resourceful is a word coined in 1807 that is a combination of *resource* and *full*. There is a myriad of resources at our disposal. Is your life full of resources, or does your "options tank" feel empty?

My goal is to awaken your ability to maneuver the resources at your disposal (money, people, talent, skills, knowledge, and time) to produce a specific outcome. This outcome will ultimately manifest the life you want while creating immense value for others.

That is why I'm here, and it's the impetus for this book.

Thanks for trusting me—and if you are an implementer, I am excited to welcome you into the millionaire's club very soon.

That day in turbulent waters taught me that our time on Earth is too short to be on autopilot. Life is not all about money, but money can give you the freedom to find your purpose. I invite you to explore your purpose as we dig into the meat of this book.

CHAPTER ONE CHECKPOINT

1. This is unapologetically a book about money.

2. With money, the sky's the limit. Without money, there is nothing but limits.

3. If you play the money game according to obsolete rules, you won't win. You need the new rules.

4. Changes in the way we make and spend money mean that the way we should invest money must also change.

5. The origin of the Have It All philosophy is rooted in a harrowing life experience that taught me to see life through a different lens.

6. To have it all means that you strive to live a full life by pushing yourself to steadily grow in three areas: health, relationships, and finances.

I have ways of
making money that you
know nothing of.

JOHN D. ROCKEFELLER

TWO

ARE YOU DOOMED?

I WAS SITTING in my tiny gray cubicle, trying to whip up the motivation to "smile and dial" the next prospect.

Anyone who has ever been a telemarketer just felt a chill run down their spine as they read that sentence. As a 22-year-old, newly married college student working a 100-percent commission job, I felt a sense of dread the moment I woke up every morning. I'd think to myself:

Am I destined to spend my days talking to people who don't want to talk to me?

I was expected to pick up that phone and dial a new number at least 100 times a day. It was torture, but I thought it was necessary. Then I was instructed to talk to people who were looking for solutions to their broken financial situations. After that, I was supposed to offer them the answers they needed. I quickly noticed something odd.

On paper, it would be easy to assume that my prospects didn't need a new financial solution. Most of my prospects:

- Graduated from college at least two or three decades prior.

- Had respectable degrees and followed society's financial game plan.

- Were faithfully stashing money into their 401(k)s.

- Were thrifty and saved money as best they could.

- Were dutifully attempting to get tax benefits by depositing money in their IRAs.

- Believed that extra cash should go toward paying off their mortgages.

Fast-forward 20 to 30 years. Some young punk was now trying to gather their financial information so his company could offer them inadequate financial solutions.

Something didn't add up.

At first, I dreaded my job because it was stressful and demeaning. Then I began to dread it for a much more disturbing reason. Every time a prospect picked up the phone and said hello, I couldn't shake the feeling that I was talking to a future version of me. I was on the same path as these desperate, aging solution-seekers.

I, too, was doing what everyone (even our parents) tells us we are supposed to do.

I had already begun forming my Have It All philosophy since that day in the riptide. And now something told me that none of this made any sense. I was about to figure out why.

My Breaking Point

When I was a kid, my parents fought about money. I have eight brothers and sisters, and there was never enough to go around. My father, a German immigrant, owned his own business and would work long hours (16-hour days were not uncommon for him).

My dad made business ownership seem like a *curse*.

He worked more than anyone I knew, but we barely had enough money to pay bills. He regularly used his own life as a cautionary tale. He would instruct me, "Son, get good grades, go to college, work for somebody else, and you'll do much better financially than working for yourself."

His grueling pace and his miniscule paycheck made for compelling arguments, and his advice seemed to be the same guidance everyone else my age was receiving. So, I believed him and worked hard to fulfill *his* plan for my life.

In high school, I did my best to get straight A's, but not every subject came easily. As a result, I'd often have to burn the midnight oil just to scrape by with a B. That wasn't good enough. My dad wasn't happy unless it was an A. He meant well—he just wanted me to have the best possible chance of getting accepted into college.

My hard work and persistence paid off because I got into a fantastic school, Brigham Young University (BYU). After I had served my two-year Christian mission, I was all set to follow my dad's game plan and secure the degree that would enable me to work for someone else my entire career.

Everyone around me was fed the same, echoing rhetoric: "Getting good grades and going to college will lead you down the road to success."

Society trains us all to be an innocuous cog in a great machine.

The cogs do all the work, while the people controlling the machine reap all the benefits. Within this system, precious few have the opportunity to live an inspiring, financially successful life.

I went to college, and, while there, I got the kind of job I thought I was supposed to have. It came with a cubicle, memos, sales leaderboards, meetings, and utter dissatisfaction.

As I sat in my little cubicle, those walls started to close in on me. *It was a gray nightmare.* I could tell from the different scribbled notes on the desk that many other cogs in the machine had come and gone before me. It was a high-turnover job, and that was no surprise—it was soul-draining work.

One day, I reached a breaking point, unable to find the courage to pick up the phone and make my next call. I decided it was an excellent time to take my lunch break. I got in my 1993 Subaru Justy (a car so small that I had to tilt my head to fit my 6'3" frame in the driver's seat) and drove home.

When I walked through the door of our postage-stamp-sized apartment, I found my young wife, Kalenn, in tears.

At first, I wasn't sure why she was crying. Maybe it was because our rent was due in five days, and we had already spent my paycheck. Perhaps it was because our college tuition was due, and we couldn't pay that either. Maybe it was because I had to give up my dream of becoming a doctor after I attempted to retake chemistry but failed.

I quickly found out why she was crying. She had gone grocery shopping and was utterly humiliated when the check she wrote had bounced. I will never forget that feeling of total failure.

My wife was home alone crying because I had failed to provide her with two of the most basic necessities in life—food and security.

The following day as my alarm went off, it hit me like a ton of bricks. I was waking up early to go to class at BYU when I *knew* that degree wouldn't break my financial chains. I was then rushing off to talk to people who were financially failing even though they were faithfully following the same path as my current trajectory.

After talking to over 1,000 people, here is what I discovered about my current track:

- Most 401(k)s hold little promise or security because they are so small.

- IRAs save you very little in taxes *and* lock your money away.

- Paying off your mortgage creates a false sense of security that doesn't last long. Eventually, you'll have to sell, remortgage, or do a reverse mortgage in a desperate attempt to squeeze out a few more years of income.

Society's game plan was massively insufficient in every way. It was time to unplug from the matrix and stop the insanity. If I did not escape, I would one day find myself on the phone with a commission-only telemarketer and wonder why I was still struggling to find financial freedom.

I finally learned the truth! Money represents freedom, but the amount of money waiting on my current path would never allow me to be truly free. I knew I needed to become a self-made millionaire, and that meant I had to blaze a new trail.

No Such Thing as Luck

The term "self-made millionaire" is both accurate and deceptive. First of all, self-made millionaires never got to where they are today entirely by themselves. There is always an unspoken army behind every success story—whether in the form of support, wisdom, encouragement, or just insight.

I get the sentiment that the term is supposed to represent. I really do. There is a certain amount of "blood, sweat, and tears," hard work, and traditional investing that becoming a "self-made millionaire" represents.

But I also think the term does a disservice to the quest to "Have It All."

In my decades-long study of the world's wealthiest people, I have never once seen an ambitious lone wolf who just so happened to *luck* into success. I've also never seen someone follow only the traditional wealth rules and actually *arrive* at their desired destination.

Instead, here's the real truth: Self-made millionaires live and operate according to a unique set of rules, particularly a specific set of superior practices related to their money.

Millionaires treat each dollar that comes across their plate differently than the rest of the world.

It's not that they have some secret "no-pain" shortcuts or just got lucky. They play by a distinctive set of *rules* that ensure their success.

But what about famous millionaires and billionaires who tell you to buck the system and be a rulebreaker? After all, Richard Branson once said, "You don't learn to walk by following rules. You learn by doing and falling over."

I don't know Mr. Branson personally, but I'll bet he's talking about breaking the rules that everyone *else* is using—the rules that lead to financial *failure* rather than *freedom*. It's the rules that keep people feeling stuck in unhappy careers, living paycheck to paycheck, and fearing they'll outlive their retirement.

Yeah, well, I wouldn't say I like those rules either.

I've made my share of mistakes, but I was also fortunate to discover early in my career that there is a *seldom-used rulebook* for attracting wealth. I'm talking about the rules that enabled me to enter my forties with fifteen years of financial freedom already behind me.

We all know the primary differences between the classes. The poor consume, while the rich invest. The poor have a fixed mindset, while the rich have a growth mindset.

But is that all there is to it?

Absolutely not.

So, where are the rich investing their money, and is that what the working class should also be doing? Aren't we all putting our paychecks into the same investments—401(k)s, IRAs, mutual funds, and money market accounts?

Hardly.

The wealthy make specific investments that set them apart in more ways than just the zeroes in their bank accounts. These underused strategies enable these men and women to become the thought leaders of our future with fresh ideas, undeniable influence, and meaningful impact.

I intend to share five investment secrets to *awaken your financial genius* and help you become a self-made millionaire. But, every life-changing revelation needs a disclaimer, so here goes mine:

> ### DISCLAIMER:
> This book will not be popular with traditional financial professionals. And they will judge you for reading it.

Financial planners don't want you to know this information (chances are, they probably don't know it themselves).

Your broker won't share this knowledge with you.

Your CPA won't recommend this financial advice.

Your older relatives may even shun this advice because it goes against what they were taught (*cognitive dissonance* is real and very powerful).

The reason is *not* that these folks want you to fail. It's merely that this information runs so far against our system's economic grain. And yet, I have never met a millionaire who wasn't using at least two of the five strategies in this book.

Although financial professionals may mean well, their livelihood comes from offering products designed to deliver significant percentages for them and minuscule gains for you.

In truth, the financial experts need you a whole lot more than you need them.

I say all of this to prepare you to be criticized for seeking out this information. Licensed financial planners may condemn it as too risky and unrealistic. But, to the wealthy, these are not foreign or dangerous ideas. They are common-sense rules that deliver seismic returns with the proper execution.

Get ready to understand the how and why behind the good luck of today's wealthy. (Spoiler: No luck is involved.)

If you are young like I was when I discovered these investments, you are ahead of the game. And if you are already mid-career or later, there is still time! I'm honored to help be a part of the wake-up call that will transform your life and secure your future.

You May Be a Genius

One of my primary goals for this book is to awaken the "financial genius" inside everyone.

Suppose you implement even a few of the five secrets in this book. Your financial outlook will be significantly better than those following society's game plan. That makes you a financial genius!

FINANCIAL GENIUS (NOUN):
An intelligent person who earns, saves, and borrows money through five specific investments that produce superior returns to fund their ideal lifestyle.

If you are 50 years or older, you may have already received an alarming financial wake-up call that you don't want to answer. You hit the snooze button, but you can only ignore a problem for so long.

Suppose you stop and calculate what you've accumulated in your 401(k), IRAs, home equity, and stock portfolio. My prediction is you'll discover the sum is not even close to what you'll need to retire—that is, if you've even saved for retirement at all.

Statistically speaking, you are probably not feeling warm and cozy about your financial future. In fact, according to *Bloomberg*: "Half of Americans have *nothing* in retirement savings."[1] CNBC also reported that according to Northwestern Mutual's most recent Planning and Progress Study:[2]

- Almost a quarter (22 percent) of Americans have less than $5,000 in savings reserved for retirement.

- Another 5 percent have between $5,000 and $24,999.

- Only 16 percent of our fellow citizens have saved $200,000 or more.

- And perhaps the most disturbing percentage, 46 percent of respondents say they don't know how much they have saved for retirement.

You don't have to be an investment finance expert to recognize that this is genuinely terrifying for most Americans. Even $200,000 (a whole pile of money compared to what most have saved) won't get you very far if you plan to live for at least a few years after you retire. You could spend a meager $40,000 a year and still only have enough money for five years of retirement.

Yikes.

Add to this the fact that people are living longer than ever, and it's a recipe for disaster. The truth is 76 percent of Americans are worried about retirement.[3] Still, they start waking up to the insufficiencies of their financial plans way too late in the ballgame.

The clock is ticking, and you're squandering your most crucial asset: time.

A *New York Post* article claimed that it's reasonable to expect people to live to over 120 years soon based on longevity trends and advances in medical technology. They call these soon-to-be long-living humans "supercentenarians."[4]

Sounds cool! That is, until you consider the fact that only 10 percent of Americans believe they have enough saved to even retire at all![5] The Employee Benefit Research Institute estimates that nearly half (41 percent) of American households with working-age adults will run out of money during retirement.[6] This means they will be forced to:

- Re-enter the workforce.

- Rely on other people or relatives or charity.

- Rely on social security as their sole income (this is already what over half of the households age 65 and older do, according to the U.S. Government Accountability Office).

Do you want to bank on the fact that you'll die shortly after retirement? And what if you don't? What then? Not to mention the exorbitant medical bills that often accompany growing older. And we haven't even brought up retirement homes, in-home care, or nursing home expenses.

When you do the math, the truth will *smack* you in the face.

I say this not to frighten you but to wake you up and correct your course before you have to push the panic button. Start now and leverage the five secrets of financial geniuses so that you'll never need to hit the panic button in the first place.

Phew! Let's all breathe a collective sigh of relief over how good "no panic button needed" sounds.

I want to help you avoid the panic button and get on the road to financial freedom sooner rather than later. The reason is that the longer you go without money, the more you sink into "scarcity mode."

When you don't operate from a place of abundance, you operate from a place of lack. This represents the difference between the "We can't afford that" mentality and the "We have the means to do what makes us happy" mentality.

People with scarcity mentalities are misers who obsessively pinch their pennies. They are worriers, constantly living in a state of anxiety. Fear replaces joy at every opportunity. The real goal should not be to pinch pennies but to work to create more than enough to retire and use the rest to build a legacy of generational wealth.

> **GENERATIONAL WEALTH (NOUN):**
> Placing your assets into a private endowment fund that continues to grow and generate cash flow for your family and others you can impact. This wealth lasts for generations, continuing to create value for those it benefits.

You can arrive at exactly where you need to be, and it doesn't have to take decades like you've been told. In four and a half years, I went from *broke* to *self-made millionaire* by using my custom roadmap.

Picture Yourself Wealthy

You need the proper roadmap, and you also need suitable investment vehicles to take you on your financial journey. Just as importantly, you are the one who needs to be driving that investment vehicle—not your CPA or your financial planner.

You are the *driver*, not just a cog in the wheel!

As the one in the driver's seat, you must also be careful to choose the right vehicle. So, what is the "right" investment vehicle? Well, in 1908, Henry Ford invented the Model T. And while it may have been an impressive vehicle in its day, I don't see any more of them on the road, do you?

If society's traditional financial solutions are the Model T, then the five investments in this book are Tesla.

Notice I didn't say Rolls-Royce. The five investments are the way of the *future*, but they are also attainable for the average person who is willing to learn. The sad thing is that right now, the world teaches people that real wealth is not within their reach. And the fact that well over 80 percent of the wealth generated goes to the world's richest 1 percent only makes that seem truer.[7]

What about the other 99 percent? Why can't they cultivate wealth?

Make no mistake—I am not a socialist. I simply believe that everyone willing to take risks and work smart should have the opportunity to create a more abundant life.

The bottom line is that broke people spend money till it's gone, and rich people invest their money and understand how to manifest superior ROIs. So, that means it's time for a lesson in ROI and how calculating it will soon become the most important action you take.

ROI Crash Course

This book is all about return on investment (ROI).

Don't let your eyes glaze over yet! There is an excellent chance you don't want to talk about math ratios right now. The thing is, there is a good chance that this same feeling keeps you from learning the ins and outs of your financial plan. It's also one of the reasons why Americans are in the mess that they're in today.

You are in charge of your financial destiny—nobody else. It's not your boss's or your spouse's job to sort out your money. It's not the custodian of your 401(k)'s job, your CPA's job, or even your financial planner's job.

You can't awaken your financial genius unless you can effectively compare investment opportunities to each other.

Your ability to do this simple math is a key to your financial freedom. So, here is the quick and dirty lowdown on ROI.

> **RETURN ON INVESTMENT (ROI): [NOUN]**
> A financial ratio used to measure how well an investment is performing. It is calculated by taking the total gain or loss on an investment and dividing that number by the total amount invested. Then, multiply the result by 100 to determine the ROI as a percentage.

There are two commonly used ROI equations—and you'll need the first one (Total ROI) to calculate the second one (Annual ROI). Once you calculate the Total ROI, you divide it by the number of years it took to achieve those gains to calculate your Annual ROI.

TOTAL ROI

$$\frac{\text{TOTAL GAIN}}{\text{TOTAL INVESTMENT}} \textbf{X 100} = \textbf{TOTAL ROI}$$

ANNUAL ROI

$$\frac{\text{TOTAL ROI}}{\text{NUMBER OF YEARS}} = \textbf{ANNUAL ROI}$$

Now, we will put our ROI formulas into practice with a simple example.

Let's say you invest $50,000 (total investment) and that investment produced a $50,000 return (gain in addition to the initial investment, also known as total gain).

Calculate the Total ROI based on those two numbers:

$$\frac{\$50,000 \text{ (gain)}}{\$50,000 \text{ (investment)}} = 1 \times 100 = 100\% \text{ TOTAL ROI}$$

Translation in English? You doubled your money. You took $50,000 and turned it into $100,000.

Now, let's say it took five years (number of years) for your $50,000 investment to earn that additional $50,000 that brought you a 100 percent Total ROI.

With that information in hand, now you can calculate your Annual ROI.

$$\frac{100 \text{ (Total ROI)}}{5 \text{ (number of years)}} = 20\% \text{ ANNUAL ROI}$$

It's easier to leave the Total ROI percentage as a whole number when calculating the Annual ROI rather than convert it back into a decimal. This simplifies the equation, so you just divide the Total ROI (as a whole number) by the number of years and the answer is your Annual ROI. Done this way, there is no need to multiply the answer by 100.

I know math isn't everyone's favorite subject, and you may have thought you escaped it forever. However, if you want to be financially free and retire without worry, there is no escaping it! Fortunately, all of the math you will find in this book never gets any more complex than this.

Here is one more example to get you warmed up to the idea of doing math again.

Let's say you invest $80,000 (total investment) and that investment produced a $160,000 return (total gain).

Calculate the Total ROI based on those two numbers:

$$\frac{\$160,000 \ (gain)}{\$80,000 \ (investment)} = 2 \times 100 = 200\% \ \text{TOTAL ROI}$$

Nice! Another solid triple-digit ROI.

Now, let's say it took just two years (number of years) for your $80,000 investment to earn that additional $160,000 that brought you a 200% Total ROI.

With that information, now you can calculate your Annual ROI:

$$\frac{200 \ (Total \ ROI)}{2 \ (number \ of \ years)} = 100\% \ \text{ANNUAL ROI}$$

ROI is a critical fundamental for creating real wealth. In the next chapter, we'll explore society's top five outdated investments, and then I'll introduce you to the five underutilized investments that the wealthy use to get wealthier through superior ROI.

When it comes to money, most people are running blind. It's time for your eyes to be opened to the truth. So, consider this your wealth wake-up call.

CHAPTER TWO CHECKPOINT

1. I was on a traditional life path, doomed to remain financially chained until I realized there had to be a better way.

2. You are squandering your biggest asset—time. But it's never too late, and you are not doomed!

3. Society's financial game plan is broken, outdated, and incapable of producing the retirement you need.

4. There is no such thing as luck when it comes to wealth. The rich just have a different plan than yours.

5. You are in charge of your financial destiny, not your parents or peers, and definitely not your traditional financial planner.

6. There is a viable solution to society's broken game plan. ROI is the key to that plan by bringing you wealth and financial freedom.

Every new beginning
comes from some other
beginning's end.

SENECA (AND SEMISONIC)

THREE

ARE YOU READY FOR THE TRUTH?

IN 1973, PRINCETON PROFESSOR Burton Malkiel made a startling claim. He wrote in his book, *A Random Walk Down Wall Street*, "A blindfolded monkey throwing darts at a newspaper's financial pages could select a portfolio that would do just as well as one carefully selected by experts."[8]

Well, it turns out that Malkiel was wrong. Monkeys can actually do *better* than the experts at picking stocks. A group of researchers from Research Affiliates proved this by gathering 100 monkeys and having them throw darts at a newspaper's stock pages. The result?

The average monkey outperformed the index by an average of 1.7 percent per year since 1964.

Of course, those who invest heavily in stocks know that they can reasonably predict ROI based on their portfolio's beta, size, and value. But think about the rest of the population—those who don't live, eat, and breathe *small-cap tilts* and *value versus growth stocks.* What do they do?

They rely on their financial expert to do the thinking for them.

If that describes you and your financial plan, it's not your fault. We trust people with the right degrees and the proper certifications for everything in life. Would you go to a five-star chef to do your taxes? Would you go to a taxidermist for open-heart surgery?

Of course not. We trust the people we are supposed to trust because that's how life works.

We live within well-defined societal constructs. However, after this book, you will know better—and when you know better, you have a responsibility to do better.

The investment vehicles that everyone should be using are not the ones that receive all the attention. I'm talking about vehicles that provide maximum ROI plus the added benefit of receiving cash flow throughout their use.

The investments that society wants you to use do *not* provide this cash flow advantage.

When you do the math, you'll see that the traditional financial game plan doesn't actually work for *anyone*—from the average American to those earning a higher income. Through the use of some calculations, you'll discover how society's plan will leave you devoid of 90 percent of the money you need to retire with confidence.

The best part about the new plan you will soon be using?

No monkeys required.

The Tunnel of Broken Dreams

Let's do a quick breakdown of society's currently accepted retirement path. I call this inferior path *The Tunnel of Broken Dreams*. These phases will likely sound familiar since there is a good chance you are currently somewhere in the tunnel yourself:

Phase 1: Get a degree and a full-time job.

First, you *must* go to college. This is the *only* possible way to earn enough money to carry out the remainder of the steps. After college, you'll need to work for someone else within a company that provides a steady income and (hopefully) benefits. This will ensure you have a regular paycheck's safety net and can provide security for your family.

Once you get this job, just keep doing it without ceasing for the next forty years. You are, of course, welcome to climb the corporate ladder and/or make lateral transitions to find a company culture that suits you best. Maybe you'll even find a company with a PlayStation in the break room and free snacks! Dare to dream.

Phase 2: Plan for your retirement.

According to this plan, real living and freedom begin at retirement. Sure, you're going to have to work extraordinarily hard for 40 plus years and scrimp and save and get that 30-year mortgage paid off in 12 years. But the good news is after you retire, you will be able to live off your investment income, savings accounts, and the no-doubt *ample* Social Security you've amassed (because everyone knows that Social Security provides us with more than enough).

Of course, a critical piece of the plan is to buy a house and pay off the note as quickly as possible. Have extra cash one month? Then why not take that surplus and make extra mortgage payments? The more money you can throw at your mortgage and keep out of higher-ROI investments, the better!

Phase 3: Live the dream forever.

Follow this rock-solid plan, and you will be able to retire with enough money to live out the rest of your days comfortably and in style. And that's it! Simple as that. Listen to the experts, work hard, do what you're told, and retire in peace. *(Note: You won't actually have enough money to retire in peace. But at least you can feel good about the fact that you did what you were told.)*

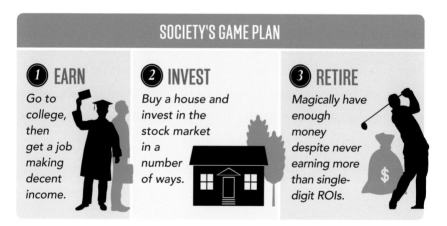

Statistics and reality have both proven this plan doesn't work, but who cares about statistics or truth, right?

So, where does this plan break down, and why does it fail for most average Americans?

While I take issue with the idea that everyone *must* go to a four-year university, the *real* problem with this plan surfaces in Phase Two. The recommended investment vehicles all only produce single-digit ROIs—and compounding single-digit ROIs just don't produce enough money.

In summary, the failure with society's plan comes down to a failure to understand and utilize ROI.

Society tells us to deposit our money into 401(k)s, IRAs, annuities, home equity, and the S&P 500. Then, we are also told to "diversify" our retirement plan. But does society's game plan really leverage diversification? Let's take a closer look by defining the word.

> **DIVERSIFICATION (NOUN):**
> Investing in a wide variety of different asset classes in multiple industries. Diversification does not mean investing in different assets (various S&P 500 stocks) within the same asset class (the stock market).

But wait—401(k)s, IRAs, annuities, and money market accounts are all just single-digit ROI derivatives of the stock market. Does that really represent diversification? *It does not.* When all of your investments produce a small ROI derived from the same place—well, that's not exactly the definition of "diversified," is it?

Failure in one asset class (such as losing money in the stock market) does not always correlate to failure in other asset classes (such as losing home values in the real estate market).

The big picture idea here is that in your lifetime, nearly every asset class is bound to experience a loss. So, true *diversification* is about spreading the risk over several asset classes. One of my mentors Ray Dalio says you have truly "de-risked" your portfolio when you have allocated your assets into at least 15 different asset classes (yes, there are that many).

THE FIVE OUTDATED INVESTMENT VEHICLES

As of now, there are five primary vehicles allowed inside The Tunnel of Broken Dreams. Although you may be familiar with these vehicles, take a moment and read these brief descriptions to understand their under-lying concepts and inherent flaws.

1. 401(k): The Front-End Loader

A 401(k) is a retirement account that allows you to divert a portion of your salary into long-term investments. In many cases, employers match their employees' contributions up to a specific percentage. The return on invest-ment (ROI) from a 401(k) is based on diversified stock market investments.

I call a 401(k) the *front-end loader* of investment vehicles because it does pick up some money for you along the way and dump it into your retire-ment years, but it's slow moving, clunky, and inefficient.

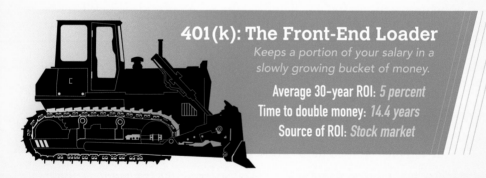

401(k): The Front-End Loader
Keeps a portion of your salary in a slowly growing bucket of money.
Average 30-year ROI: *5 percent*
Time to double money: *14.4 years*
Source of ROI: *Stock market*

Here are the relevant ROI stats you need to know about the average 401(k):

- The 30-year average ROI is 5 percent.

- Returns are based on the stock market.

- The time it takes to double your money is 14.4 years.

After a sophisticated analysis of 401(k) performance over thirty years, experts say a 5 percent return appears to be an accurate number to use for planning purposes.[9] Add to this that Fidelity Investments says a good rule of thumb is to *have eight times your current salary saved for retirement.*[10]

So, that means if you are 60 years old and make $100,000 a year, your 401(k) balance (if you are relying on it to be a significant portion of your retirement nest egg) should be at least $800,000.

Unfortunately, reality once again rears its ugly head to show us this is rarely the case.

The average 401(k) balance for Americans in their sixties (and supposedly ready to retire) is just $93,400.[11] So much for the "eight times your salary" rule.

And how does that make sense anyway? What kind of person would even feel comfortable with only eight years' worth of salary saved? What happens if you live longer? What about the fact that you are expected to live on *less*, even though retirees often spend *more* due to increased medical costs, travel, and other expenses? So, the question becomes:

Should I put a portion of my salary into a 401(k)? I think you know my answer, but here are some other questions you need to be asking yourself:

- Is it a good idea to depend on an investment vehicle whose single-digit ROI leaves me approximately 93 percent short of my goal?

- What is the benefit of a company match earning single digits that I can't touch or re-invest unless I leave the company?

- How do I feel knowing my 401(k) is loaded with hidden fees like administrative fees, investment advisory fees, and expense ratio fees?

- Do I feel confident knowing that just 6.8 percent of Americans can rely on their 401(k) as their sole source of retirement income next to Social Security and pensions?[12]

The bottom line: Right now, over half (56 percent) of U.S. workers have a 401(k).[13] Yet, studies also reveal that almost half of the people who have a 401(k) will struggle to maintain their standard of living in retirement.[14] Something just doesn't add up here.

2. Traditional IRA: The Bicycle

IRAs (both traditional and Roth) are standard, popular vehicles that serve as "tax-advantaged" investment accounts. Returns from an IRA are based on diversified investments in the stock market. I refer to an IRA as a *bicycle with a flower basket.* It's cute—and you can plod casually along with your little basket of pristine pre-tax dollars, happy that you saved a few bucks on taxes in exchange for a single-digit return.

Traditional IRA: The Bicycle
Allows you to carry a little basket of pre-tax dollars with you into the future.

Average 30-year ROI: *7 percent*
Time to double money: *12 years*
Source of ROI: *Stock market*

The difference between the two main types of IRAs is contribution timing:

With a *traditional IRA*, you make contributions with pre-tax dollars (and pay income tax when you withdraw the funds later). The basic idea with the timing is to take advantage of the fact that when you retire, you'll find yourself in a lower tax bracket than you were in pre-retirement.

With a *Roth IRA*, you make contributions with after-tax dollars. This means you can receive distributions "tax-free" and penalty-free at your discretion after the fact, as long as you meet conditions such as being a certain age.

Here are the relevant stats you need to know about the average IRA:

- The 30-year average ROI is 7 to 10 percent.

- Returns are based on the stock market.

- The time it takes to double your money is 12 years.

According to experts, you can expect between 7 to 10 percent average annual returns. However, with inflation, it's wise to be more conservative and use 7 percent ROI in your calculations.

CPAs and financial planners recommend utilizing an IRA to save money on taxes, as mentioned previously. Here's a simple example of how that works with a traditional IRA:

> If you make $60,000 per year and pay 15 percent in federal taxes, then putting $3,000 a year into a traditional IRA would lower taxable income to $57,000 and save 15 percent of $3,000, or a total savings of only $450. Keep in mind that the $3,000 will still be subject to taxation at the time of withdrawal (but fingers crossed, you will be at a lower tax bracket).

So, the question becomes:

Should I use an IRA for the minor tax benefits and single-digit ROI? An IRA can save you a few dollars in taxes, but ask yourself the following questions:

- Does it make sense to pick up minor tax savings now on a traditional IRA when I am still going to be taxed when I withdraw it later?

- Should I be depending on a secondary single-digit ROI investment vehicle that leaves me far short of my retirement goals?

- What multi-digit investment opportunities am I missing out on by locking my money in an IRA that, in some cases, tacks on a 10 percent penalty if I try to access it?

The bottom line: In the end, an IRA is great for two things: a single-digit ROI and a guarantee that you will not have enough money to retire comfortably.

3. Annuity: The Ice Cream Truck

An *annuity* is a contract that makes regular payments to you either now or in the future. Returns from an annuity are based on diversified investments in the stock market. I call it the *ice cream truck* of finance vehicles because it slowly dolls out the goods in bite-sized pieces. It will also stop making its rounds after the ice cream is gone.

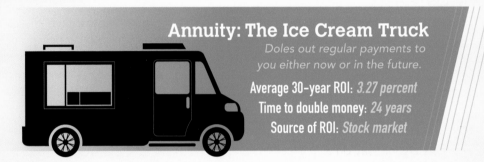

Annuity: The Ice Cream Truck
Doles out regular payments to you either now or in the future.
Average 30-year ROI: *3.27 percent*
Time to double money: *24 years*
Source of ROI: *Stock market*

Here are the relevant ROI stats you need to know about annuities:

- The 30-year average ROI is 3.27 percent.

- Returns are based on the stock market.

- The time it takes to double your money is 24 years.

Your financial planner may recommend consolidating all 401(k)s, IRAs, and other similar investment accounts into an annuity when you retire. Essentially, your money gets locked into secure stock market-based investments that allow the financial planner to guarantee an annual dividend that serves as your "fixed income." So, the question becomes:

Should I use an annuity to guarantee a fixed income? It's nice to have a known amount of guaranteed income, but ask yourself the following questions:

- Is a 3.27 percent dividend sufficient to help me achieve all of my financial goals?

- How do I feel knowing that the average man hits his peak annual earnings of $95,000 by age 53? This means I would need to save

$2.9 million for an annuity to match that same income post-retirement (more on this figure in a few pages).[15]

- Do I think this is a realistic savings goal, considering the average retirement savings for workers in their sixties is just $170,000?

- Would I be interested in only needing a third of that amount to retire by finding a way to significantly outperform an annuity?

I hope you answer yes to that last question because it's why this book exists.

The bottom line: The Transamerica Center for Retirement Studies reports that the median retirement savings amount for U.S. workers in their sixties is $172,000.[16] If you were to annuitize this at an annual dividend of 3.27 percent, you would receive a mere $468.70 each month as fixed income.

There is *no way on earth* that a fixed income of less than $500 a month is sufficient to fund a carefree retirement.

4. S&P 500: The Tractor

The Standard & Poor's (S&P) 500 is a market-capitalization-weighted index that tracks the stocks of 500 of the largest U.S. publicly traded companies. I call the S&P 500 the *tractor* of investment vehicles because it's reliable for single-digit returns but slow and boring as heck to watch.

S&P 500: The Tractor
Slowly tracks the stocks of the largest U.S. publicly traded companies.
Average 30-year ROI: *7.96 percent*
Time to double money: *9 years*
Source of ROI: *Stock market*

Here are the relevant ROI stats you need to know about the S&P 500:

- The 30-year average ROI is 7.96 percent.

- Returns are based on the stock market.

- The time it takes to double your money is 9 years.

Essentially, your ROI from the S&P 500 is the average growth of the top 500 publicly traded companies in America. And the 7.96 percent ROI is calculated by looking at the returns from 500 stocks since 1957.

Should I rely on the S&P 500 as an investment strategy? It's great to earn a solid ROI from the 500 most successful companies in America, but ask yourself the following questions:

- Suppose I already have 401(k)s, IRAs, and annuities based on the stock market. Does it make sense to have yet another single-digit investment that is also based on the stock market?

- Why would I want to invest my money in a vehicle that requires decades (to account for market fluctuations) to create an average single-digit ROI?

- What if I need to liquidate my stock portfolio when the market is down? Wouldn't it erase years of growth and end up in the red?

The bottom line: There is nothing wrong with investing in the stock market. But at this point, all four of the *accepted investment vehicles* have been based on the stock market and deliver meager, single-digit ROIs.

Things are starting to feel a little redundant and uncreative, aren't they? And yet, traditional financial advisors call this "being diversified."

5. Home Equity: The Antique Car

Your *home equity* is your home's value that is the difference between the home's fair market value (determined by appraisal) and the out-standing balance of all liens on the property. When you take out a home equity loan or home equity line of credit (often referred to as a HELOC), you are using your home's equity as collateral for the loan.

I call your home equity the *antique car* of the traditional investment fleet because it's nice to look at and everyone enjoys owning it and bragging about it. But also like an antique car, it doesn't actually take you anywhere.

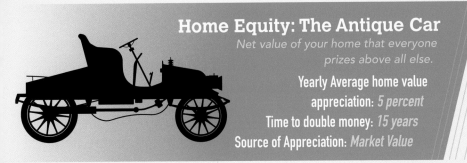

Home Equity: The Antique Car
Net value of your home that everyone prizes above all else.

Yearly Average home value appreciation: *5 percent*
Time to double money: *15 years*
Source of Appreciation: *Market Value*

Here are the relevant stats you need to know about home equity:

- The average home value appreciation is 4.65 percent per year (comes from average home value increases in the U.S. since 1963).

- The time it takes to double your money is 15 years.

I consider home equity to be an investment vehicle because it will comprise the lion's share of the majority of Americans' net worth by retirement. People love seeing their home equity increase, and that's understandable. It's their "one of a kind" commodity—that rare antique in their asset column of which they are most proud.

The home equity ROI may appear smaller compared to the other investments discussed. Just remember that appreciation is not calculated on the money you invest, but rather the growth of the home and property's total value. To further explain:

The median home price in America in 2020 was $320,000.[17] With an average annual appreciation of 4.65 percent, that equates to $14,880 in growth per year. Therefore, in reality, your home equity growth usually *outperforms* your other investments over time because this "investment" isn't starting with a zero balance. It's starting with the value of your home when you buy it.

Should I view my home equity as an investment? Of course. Still, many people don't consider their home equity to be an "investment" compared to the more traditional market-based investments such as a 401(k) and an IRA. It's also hard to convince anyone with any common sense that a home equity *loan* is an investment—especially if you are *forced* to take out a home equity loan to use as retirement income.

It's great to earn a solid ROI on your home and work towards paying it off, but ask yourself the following questions:

- Even though my home increases in value over time, how can I call it an investment when it's more like a *liability*? It costs money every month and does not produce an income!

- If my home equity produces most of my assets in life, why am I not buying a lot more houses?

- Suppose my home equity grows by $200,000 over 20 years. Why not buy four more houses to produce an additional $1,000,000 in personal net worth?

The bottom line: It pains me to hear people talk about their "greatest investment" (their home) but then not amplify what works (buy more properties). If owning a home is the best way to grow your net worth, then why not do more of what works?

DEVIL'S ADVOCATE

"I'm happy that you've been able to buy tons of houses over the years, Kris. Really, I'm thrilled for you, man. But I have no idea how to buy houses that actually make money without creating a nightmare of work and extra hassle."

I get it! In Chapter Six, I will explain why it's possible to get into the real estate game in a way that is turnkey and automated and eliminates the undesirables (such as becoming a landlord).

Don't Get Stuck in the Tunnel

A fleet of nothing-but-single-digit ROI investment vehicles gives me all the wrong emotions. The sheer thought fills me with the same panic I felt when I worked that commission-only telemarketing job inside four tiny gray walls.

Let me be clear: There's nothing wrong with a single-digit ROI unless *all* of your investment vehicles produce single-digit returns. If your investments are all earning single-digit ROIs, it becomes mathematically impossible for them to manifest your financial dreams. What looks so safe and risk-free will end up being the riskiest choice you could have ever made.

By investing in society's accepted investment vehicles, you will not have enough financial fuel to reach your retirement destination. You'll be left stalled in the tunnel, with no end in sight.

Despite the way it might look, I'm not here to wage war against society's investment vehicles. I am here to get you to think differently. To think bigger. To break you out of old programming so that you can discover something better.

Rather than take my word for it, in the next section, we'll do some straightforward math to empower you to understand: 1) what you already have, 2) what you need, and 3) the best plan to get you there. It's *your* retirement, and that means you need to take ownership of it and gain the confidence that only comes from educating yourself.

One of my passions in life is to provide a financial game plan that can predict when you will become financially free with far more accuracy than society's defunct plan. In fact, I would go so far as to say that society's plan, in many cases, is a total sham because it isn't a "plan" at all.

Plans are supposed to get you to an end goal, to a target, or to a desired result. Yet, society's financial plan accomplishes exactly none of those things.

> Should you find yourself in a chronically leaking boat, energy devoted to changing vessels is likely to be more productive than energy devoted to patching leaks.
>
> WARREN BUFFET

Your retirement path should not be riddled with ambiguities and guesswork. You should be able to look at your current financial strategy and determine whether it is sufficient to create the future you want.

Once I did this simple math, I changed my strategy. Within a few years, I became financially free. Today I'm earning double, triple, and quadruple-digit ROIs. I also live with confidence and joy because I am making more than enough money to live my dream lifestyle, stash away cash, and have it all.

Rule of 72: Your Valuable Vetting Tool

It's time to further awaken your financial genius! For today, that starts with teaching you the **Rule of 72.** This rule helps you understand how long it will take for you to double your money and how your money compounds over time.

I call the Rule of 72 my "financial sniff check." It's a very simple litmus test to quickly determine whether the investment you are considering is **fresh** (will help you achieve financial freedom *when* you want it) or **rotten** (is an inefficient or outright unwise way to grow your money).

Here are the basics: Divide 72 by the annual interest rate (denoted in the formula as R) to determine the approximate time required to double the investment (represented in the formula as T).

THE RULE OF 72

INTEREST RATE

$$72 \div R$$

YEARS TO DOUBLE

$$=$$

$$T$$

The Rule of 72 is an easy and practical way to calculate how long (T) an investment will take to double if compounded at a fixed annual rate of interest (R). The ultimate goal of the Rule of 72 is to show the power of compounding interest (a principle that Albert Einstein once called the most powerful force in the world).

COMPOUNDING INTEREST (NOUN):
A powerful way to earn interest on the interest you receive, which multiplies your money at an accelerating rate.

Speaking of Einstein, he is often credited with being the architect of the Rule of 72, although Luca Pacioli, a renowned mathematician from Italy, is reportedly the first person who appeared to reference the rule in his 1494 book on mathematics called *Summa de arithmetica*.

It turns out that while determining compounding interest the long way is an extremely complicated equation, someone (maybe it was Pacioli, maybe it was Einstein) found a cheat code! They discovered that dividing 72 by the annual interest rate always leads to the right amount of time it takes to double an investment.

In this way, the number 72 in the world of finance holds the same mysterious magical power as Archimedes' constant, otherwise known as "pi" or 3.14.

Fortunately, that's about as deep as we need to dive into the history of mathematics for this book. And even better, the math we will be doing is straightforward and easy to calculate!

Ready for some easy math? No guesswork required. I'll walk you through step by step; each calculation takes just seconds. So, open the calculator app on your smartphone, and let's do some basic calculations.

EXAMPLE #1
Savings Account with 0.25 percent Yearly ROI

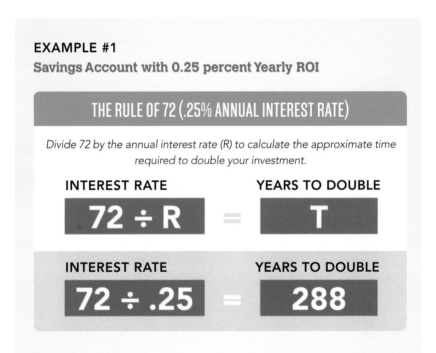

THE RULE OF 72 (.25% ANNUAL INTEREST RATE)

Divide 72 by the annual interest rate (R) to calculate the approximate time required to double your investment.

INTEREST RATE		YEARS TO DOUBLE
72 ÷ R	=	T

INTEREST RATE		YEARS TO DOUBLE
72 ÷ .25	=	288

When we were kids, we learned that a bank account is where you put money to keep it safe. Today, many adults still keep money safe in the bank and earn no more than a 0.25 percent ROI. So, let's say you have $10,000 in a savings account, earning an annual fixed interest rate of 0.25 percent. How many years will it take to double your money?

$$72 ÷ 0.25 = 288 \text{ years}$$

With a single-digit ROI at 0.25 percent, that $10,000 will take a ridiculous 288 years to double and become $20,000.

DEVIL'S ADVOCATE

"But Kris, I wasn't putting my money in the bank expecting it to grow into anything. I was just trying to keep it safe."

Did you know that money loses 2 to 3 percent of its value every year? When you store it in a place earning less than 2 or 3 percent, it actually creates a *negative* return. Ironically, money itself provides such an inferior store of value because when this country needs more money, we just print more money. This causes the value of the dollar to drop slowly over time—and that is the underlying cause of inflation, which has averaged 3.1 percent over the last century.

We print money like it's coupons for Wendy's, and even more concerning, our money is backed by … basically nothing. Even when the dollar was backed by gold, the U.S. government would adjust the gold-to-dollar ratio with regularity, essentially muting any effect of the currency's gold backing.

But don't worry because in Chapter Five, I will show you a safer place to stash your cash reserve that earns a minimum of 5 percent a year!

EXAMPLE #2
401(k) with 5 percent Yearly ROI

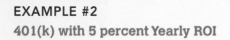

THE RULE OF 72 (5% ANNUAL INTEREST RATE)

Divide 72 by the annual interest rate (R) to calculate the approximate time required to double your investment.

INTEREST RATE		YEARS TO DOUBLE
$72 \div R$	=	T

INTEREST RATE		YEARS TO DOUBLE
$72 \div 5$	=	14.4

Now, let's do the math on your 401(k). If you invest $10,000 at an annual fixed interest rate of 5 percent, how many years will it take to double your money?

$$72 \div 5 = 14.4 \text{ years}$$

With a single-digit ROI at 5 percent (your socially acceptable investment), that same $10,000 will take roughly 14.4 years to double.

EXAMPLE #3
Blended Returns with 8 percent Yearly ROI

THE RULE OF 72 (8% ANNUAL INTEREST RATE)

Divide 72 by the annual interest rate (R) to calculate the approximate time required to double your investment.

INTEREST RATE		YEARS TO DOUBLE
72 ÷ R	=	**T**

INTEREST RATE		YEARS TO DOUBLE
72 ÷ 8	=	**9**

Now let's blend some single-digit investment choices, such as the S&P 500 with an IRA, for an average return of 8 percent.

$$72 \div 8 = 9 \text{ years}$$

With a single-digit ROI at 8 percent, that same $10,000 will take roughly nine years to double.

You've already elevated your financial genius by being able to compare these three options side by side. Now, let's look at these three common financial choices (savings, 401(k), and blended single digit returns) graphically to see their growth over 20 years.

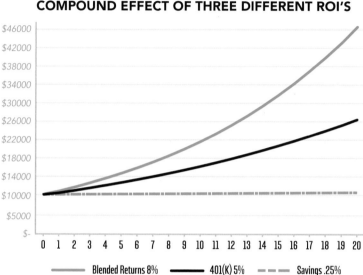

COMPOUND EFFECT OF THREE DIFFERENT ROI'S

Blended Returns 8% — 401(K) 5% - - - Savings .25%

Even from a quick glance, it's easy to see how the higher ROI of 8 percent begins to grow *exponentially* faster and outperforms the 5 percent ROI and certainly the 0.25 percent ROI.

I want to pause for a minute to reflect on the word *exponential.*

There's a reason why Albert Einstein (allegedly) declared *compounding interest* to be the greatest financial invention of all time, and you can see the logic in that graph. The savings account earning 0.25 percent will take 288 years to double a $10,000 pile of money.

On the other hand, it will only take nine years to double that same pile of money at an 8 percent yearly ROI!

You're Getting Left in the Dust

Every job trades time for dollars. You put in x number of hours, and you get x amount of money in return, or what I call "financial fuel." When you pump your hard-earned financial fuel into outdated investment vehicles, you find they don't go very far, and here's why ....

On average, you have a 40-year working life. How many times can you double your money in 40 years? Let's assume you're like most of the country, and your money is earning an average of 6 percent. That means your money doubles every 12 years (according to the Rule of 72):

$$72 \div 6\% \; ROI = 12 \; years \; to \; double \; your \; money$$

If you work for 40 years, how many times can your money double if it takes 12 years to do so?

You can double your money, at most, maybe three times.

Meanwhile, all of these financial planners are coasting along on the open highway, making money hand over fist by managing *your* money. Your money is stuck in a traffic jam making other people money.

In short, you're getting left in the dust.

But before we go any further, I need to ask you an important question:

Have you ever thought about how much money you actually need to retire comfortably?

Most people save for retirement without ever having an answer to this all-important question.

How in the world can you reach a destination if you don't even know what it is? You can only know if your financial game plan is adequate once you have a *concrete* and *defined* financial retirement goal.

Remember earlier when I said you would need $2.9 million that earns a guaranteed 3 percent to produce $95,000 of interest each year of retirement? Let's just assume for a moment that $2.9 million is your goal. Here's an analogy:

You are in Los Angeles (with no money), but you need to get to New York City (where the $2.9 million awaits). You go to work and trade your time for money, and each dollar you save over what you spend goes towards that $2.9 million.

This is the absolute *slowest* way to amass $2.9 million, and, frankly, it's like trying to walk to New York City. You have no vehicle, and you will never save up $2.9 million by putting a few spare dollars under the mattress with every paycheck.

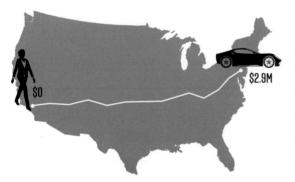

When you put your dollars in a vehicle like a 401(k), your money starts to move a little faster, and the results are far better than stuffing cash under your mattress.

However, is a 401(k) or the other vehicles we've discussed ultimately the right pick to get to your $2.9 million destination?

Maybe if you lived for several hundred years. But in this life? Never.

Remember, reality and research tell us that the average amount a person takes with him or herself into retirement is a paltry $172,000 (only 6 percent of $2.9 million). If you are serious about getting to New York and having $2.9 million or more, then you need to consider two things:

1. **The Right Investment Vehicles.** If you use slow-moving vehicles, you may never make it to your financial destination. You need faster vehicles.

2. **High Performing Financial Fuel.** You also need your money to earn a notable return. You traded your time for it, and now you need to put it to work. The fuel is your ROI. With a low ROI, your money isn't working hard enough. With a higher ROI, your financial fuel will take you further.

THE FIVE TRADITIONAL INVESTMENTS: OLD & SLOW

The Front-End Loader
401(K) earning 5%

The Bicycle
IRA earning 7%

The Tractor
S&P 500 earning 8%

The Antique Car
Home Equity earning 4.65%

The Ice Cream Truck
Annuity earning 3.27%

It comes down to this: If you were in a race for financial freedom, which of these investment vehicles would you want to ensure your future?

In nearly 20 years of interviewing over 10,000 people, I have yet to meet a single person who chose these inferior vehicles and got even halfway to $2.9 million or more. You will *not* have enough money to retire when you use slow, outdated investment vehicles. Not to mention, you're going to run out of financial fuel long before you get to New York City. And I hate to break it to you, but The Tunnel of Broken Dreams is fresh out of filling stations.

Bottom line: It's time to upgrade your investment fleet and power them all with superior financial fuel.

Get Ready for High Performance

The time has come to talk about upgraded vehicles that give you a real shot at achieving financial freedom.

My study of the wealthy revealed these five vehicles. My mentorship with wealthy influencers helped me implement these five investments into my personal *Financial Freedom Roadmap*. And my friendships with millionaires and billionaires continues to accelerate and celebrate my results and the impact they have on the world—including you!

We are going to spend plenty of time breaking down each of these. But for now, let's use the Sports Car (double-digit ROI) and revisit the Rule of 72 and compounding interest.

EXAMPLE #4
Investment with 25 percent Yearly ROI

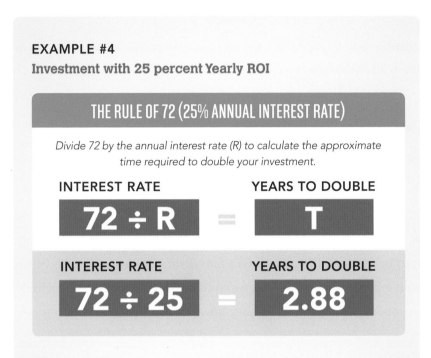

THE RULE OF 72 (25% ANNUAL INTEREST RATE)

Divide 72 by the annual interest rate (R) to calculate the approximate time required to double your investment.

INTEREST RATE		YEARS TO DOUBLE
72 ÷ R	=	T

INTEREST RATE		YEARS TO DOUBLE
72 ÷ 25	=	2.88

Since you've already awoken your financial genius, this should be easy. Imagine for a moment that you are earning 25 percent from your investments. How many years would it take to double your money given the same $10,000 starting investment we used earlier?

72 ÷ 25 = 2.88 years

With a double-digit ROI at 25 percent, that same $10,000 that would take 288 years to double in a savings account will double in 2.88 years!

Let's take that math a step further, so you can really start to see the power of ROI: A 25 percent ROI will grow 27 times more money than a 6 percent ROI over 20 years. *Want to look at that graphically?* You should, because it's exciting! Check out the growth of $10,000 over 20 years at 6 percent versus 25 percent.

6 PERCENT VS. 25 PERCENT ROI OVER 20 YEARS

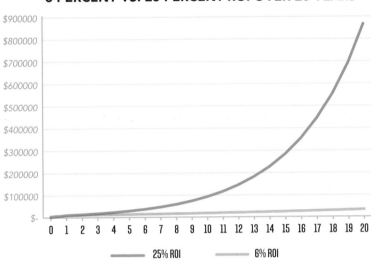

If you put $10,000 into the gas tank of a 6 percent ROI investment vehicle over 20 years, it will produce just over $32,0000.

On the other hand, if you put $10,000 into the gas tank of a 25 percent ROI investment vehicle over 20 years, it will produce almost $870,000.

Imagine the power of 25 percent ROI or more. Imagine the power of building your multi-million-dollar financial game plan to turn your dreams into reality. In Part Two, I will teach you all about your new financial fleet of investment vehicles and what they can and will do for you:

1. *First Comes Security.* You'll learn how to prepare for security the right way. I'll show you my single-digit ROI investment vehicle—the *only* one I use—that will help you establish security for the present.

> **Money makes money. And the money that money makes, makes money.**
>
> BENJAMIN FRANKLIN

2. *Next Comes Speed.* You will then discover the three invest-ment vehicles that are like race cars. We're talking about traveling cross-country from LA to NYC faster and in style. These are the double-digit, triple-digit, and quadruple-digit ROIs.

3. *Then Comes Exponential Growth.* Finally, I will introduce you to my ultimate financial shortcut—infinite ROI. It's like flying in your own private jet! After all, the fastest way from LA to NYC is in the air. Still, all the vehicles in my arsenal are far superior to society's broken-down invest-ment vehicles.

We have reached the end of Part One! The goal of the first three chapters was to expose society's broken plan and to preview a new plan designed to fully awaken the financial genius that is already inside you.

You may not feel like a genius yet, but, believe it or not, you now have the foundation you need to more readily understand the *Financial Freedom Roadmap* in the next chapter that lays the groundwork for the rest of the book.

Are you ready? Then let's rev up the engine and step on the gas because your new financial fleet is going to leave society's slow-moving invest-ment vehicles in that dusty old tunnel.

> ### The best way to predict your future is to create it.
> ABRAHAM LINCOLN

CHAPTER THREE CHECKPOINT

1. Society tells us we have to trust the "experts" and discourages bucking the system that has been in place for far too long.

2. The Tunnel of Broken Dreams is a sad place where five slow investment vehicles (401(k)s, IRAs, annuities, S&P 500, and home equity) run out of gas and leave nothing behind but regret.

3. The Rule of 72 is a vetting tool to show whether you are being too conservative as well as how far your current investment vehicles will get you.

4. When you apply the Rule of 72, you'll see that single-digit ROI can't earn money fast enough to reach your financial destination.

5. Compounding is the most tremendous financial force in the universe. That is, as long as you're compounding something more exciting than a single-digit ROI.

6. Diversification is key! In other words, you want a fleet with a wide range of ROIs (from single-digit to infinite ROIs).

PART TWO

AWAKENING YOUR FINANCIAL GENIUS

**If you can't describe
what you are doing
as a process,
you don't know
what you're doing.**

W. EDWARDS DEMING

FOUR

THE FINANCIAL
FREEDOM ROADMAP

THE WEALTHIEST PEOPLE in the world are rarely the most intelligent. I'm no exception to this.

They don't necessarily have the most enormous IQs. They definitely don't have the highest degrees from the most prestigious institutions. The most successful people are not smarter or "better" than everyone else. Do you know the one big thing they have that the rest of the world doesn't?

They have systems. *For everything.*

Think about the last time you tried to assemble some IKEA furniture. Do you remember how you felt when you dumped that box out, and countless pieces spilled all over the floor? There is possibly no worse feeling in the world (okay, there are worse feelings, but it's a bad one).

Then you opened up that instruction booklet and saw the steps. You were overwhelmed but also relieved that someone else figured out how to assemble it, so you didn't have to. All of those pieces fit together, and, in the end, after exerting some effort and following the steps in order, you created a functional finished product.

Without that instruction book (or roadmap, if you will), that pile of raw materials would end up in the garbage.

Well, guess what? That's the way your money feels right now. *It feels like garbage.* It desperately wants you to find a system for investing in your financial future and implement it—but right now? Your money just feels underappreciated and undervalued.

Maybe you're thinking, "But Kris, I've never even had enough surplus cash to be able to hurt its feelings!"

That may be true—but it's not going to be true for much longer. Follow my *Financial Freedom Roadmap*, and a time will come when you won't need to be shopping at IKEA or assembling your own furniture (unless you want to).

I delayed all forms of financial gratification for five years at the start of my journey, and then a time came when I could literally buy anything I wanted.

On the other hand, I haven't changed my lifestyle in the last ten years even though my net worth continues to increase. One of my real estate mentors, Dolf De Roose, said that his ultimate goal was *to own nothing and rent everything when he needed it.* Aside from my estate and a few nice vehicles, I essentially own nothing. I'll use a private driver to take me around when I don't feel like driving (or can't trust myself to not use my cell phone behind the wheel). I also travel in style and visit the nicest resorts, and I can enjoy private planes and helicopters when needed without actually buying them.

The lifestyle I have crafted gives me incredible variety and frankly is far less expensive because I don't get attached to *things*. I am obsessed with making epic memories with the people I love, not the objects I own.

Aside from travel, my favorite thing to spend money on is mentorship from the world's leading authorities. I maximize my learning and life experiences when I engage with the best of the best in every field. Why have home cooked meals when a personal chef can make healthy food taste exquisite? If you struggle at the gym, then why not work with the best personal trainer in the area?

My wife and I also decided to take our four kids' education into our own hands and hire private teachers to educate them according to *our* standards. My financial roadmap is what enabled us to do this. And can you guess who is teaching my children about money? It's certainly not the part-time assistant football coach/economics teacher.

Even more than a goal to own nothing and rent when needed, my underlying goal has always been to believe I actually *can* have it all. Why not think big? So, before we begin, I need you to do the following:

Set aside any *hint* of a limited mindset, doubt, or skepticism and start thinking bigger.

You may be approaching things from a scarcity mindset, as in, *I don't have the money to invest in any financial vehicle, let alone the ones that Kris is going to teach me.* Instead, I want you to think, *I will find the money to set aside because my future and my legacy depend on it.*

In this chapter, I introduce my system for becoming a multi-millionaire. But here's the *crazy* part. Because of what I know about human nature, I also know that 95 percent of the people who read this will never implement the system.

Why is that?

I don't want to turn this into a psychology book, but let's just say that *taking action* is not a strength found in most people's wheelhouse. I hope you are the exception. I want you to join the small percentage of people who develop systems to run their lives. Better yet:

I want you to become a person who saves time by finding and implementing *proven* systems and procedures.

The inability or unwillingness to take action is why I can freely give away my system for becoming a multi-millionaire and know that few will act on my advice. There will still be many who sit around complaining about how the wealthy must know some "secrets" that no one else does.

No, they don't.

The wealthy just use proven systems for making money. Life functions well when you have systems and processes in place. And the sooner you realize this, the faster you will have it all.

Ready to learn my system for exponentially growing your wealth? I hope so. And unlike an IKEA coffee table, there is no assembly required.

And Then My System Happened

Remember my gray cubicle nightmare job? Fast forward a few short years and picture a 26-year-old me gazing out a storybook window at a rolling green golf course amidst the luxury of my own custom-built mansion.

What the heck happened?!

My system happened.

I started having success with a few investments, and I began developing my theory of wealth. That theory and my successes ultimately became the system you are about to learn.

It started with aggressively saving money through making personal financial sacrifices. Then I poured my savings into investment vehicles. Those investments created a monthly positive cash flow. I took that cash flow and put it right back into more investments.

I did this repeatedly until four years later, when I had a $12,000 surplus each month after paying my bills. Every subsequent month, the excess cash grew until it became utterly ridiculous to keep going to my traditional job.

I turned my wealth creation into a systematic machine that took on a life of its own. The "secrets" that made all this possible were simple:

- I reserved money for investing.

- I invested that reserve into high-ROI investment vehicles.

- I converted those investments into cash flow to reinvest and fund my lifestyle.

These three steps (set to repeat indefinitely) became my Financial Freedom Roadmap for exponentially increasing my wealth each year. There are two core components of the roadmap:

1. **The Strategy.** My *Compounding ROI Investments Strategy* leverages the five core vehicles required to build wealth.

2. **The System.** I use the strategy as the foundation for my *Three-Step Wealth Creation System*—reserve, invest, and convert cash.

The path to financial security is not hidden—study the rich, and you'll discover this is how they "do wealth." In the following two sections, we'll break down both essential elements in my roadmap.

The Strategy: Compounding ROI Investments

In the last chapter, we tore apart five inadequately slow investments found within the Tunnel of Broken Dreams. I also previewed five exciting new investment vehicles that feature ROIs ranging from single-digit to infinite. Then we discussed *compounding* and how powerful it is.

See how much financial genius you've already awakened?

You know exactly what's coming next and what vehicles and destinations make up the roadmap. So now, let's formally define the strategy.

> **COMPOUNDING ROI INVESTMENT STRATEGY (NOUN):**
> A system used by financial geniuses consisting of five vehicles for building wealth. Leveraging all five and reinvesting the surplus produces a compound effect so powerful that you create a lifetime of wealth within a few years.

It's time to meet your new fleet that is an integral part of the plan— the vehicles that are well equipped to keep you riding from LA (insufficient savings) to NYC (ample savings) in comfort, style, and class.

YOUR NEW FINANCIAL FLEET

The Armored Truck:
Financial Reserve Vehicle

Single-digit ROI

The first vehicle in the financial fleet is your armored truck full of investment funds. It's the place to stash your cash! With the appropriate *Aggressive Savings Strategy* or A.S.S. (more on that in a minute), you will be able to store reserves in a specific account. The average bank account may produce a 0.1 percent return, but this is a more intelligent account that delivers a yield between 5 and 7 percent annually. You trade your time for money every day—but what have you done with that money so far? When invested this way, your money starts working for you, not the other way around. Ultimately, you will use your reserve vehicle as a smart holding tank for your money (financial fuel) as you prepare to fill up the tanks of your new investment fleet.

The Sports Car:
Passive Income Vehicle

Double-digit ROI

The second vehicle in the financial fleet is your passive income investment vehicle that produces double-digit ROI through real estate. I'll explain how it's possible to tap into passive, turnkey real estate investments that can consistently deliver an annual ROI of around 25 percent. You can create as much as 27 times more wealth than conventional retirement vehicles by utilizing this investment. This vehicle is what allows you to amass millions throughout your working life. It won't create financial freedom overnight, but it will ensure that, in time, you can get there.

The Race Car: Asymmetric Risk/Stock Market Philosophy Vehicle

Triple-digit ROI

Your fleet's third vehicle is an asymmetric risk investment that produces triple-digit ROI through implementing a unique stock market philosophy. The stock market intimidates many people, but it doesn't have to be complicated.

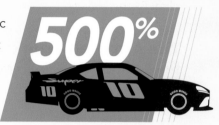

I don't like 401(k)s and IRAs, but that doesn't mean I don't like the stock market. Let me be clear: The only thing I dislike about society's vehicles are boring, single-digit ROIs. I *love* owning a piece of the future through carefully vetted companies with incredible upsides. Even better, market returns are passive (like the second vehicle), so they don't rob you of valuable time.

The Formula 1 Car: Active Income Vehicle

Quadruple-digit ROI

Your fleet's fourth vehicle is an active income vehicle that pro-

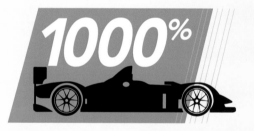

duces quadruple-digit ROI through smart business investments. This vehicle requires minimal time investment for maximum return. It also acts as an accelerator to help you achieve goals in *years* instead of *decades*.

The Private Jet: Strategic Partnership Vehicle

Infinite ROI

The fifth vehicle in your fleet is the strategic partnership vehi-

cle that produces infinite ROI. You generate infinite ROI when leveraging the power of other people's money. This strategy is the ultimate accelerator for achieving your biggest results in the shortest period.

As we continue, you will further awaken your financial genius and learn how to produce results far exceeding those promised by society's game plan. By the end of this book, you'll understand how to leverage each of these vehicles to harness the power of Compounding ROI Investments.

Of course, a strategy is only as good as the system in which it is integrated. Fortunately, I have developed such a system.

The System: Three-Step Wealth Creation

Through my system, you will learn how to properly reserve, invest, and convert cash into wealth via the following steps:

- *Step 1.* **Reserve** *financial fuel for your fleet.* You need an *Aggressive Savings Strategy,* or A.S.S., to reserve 20 percent of what you make for the investments that build your wealth.

- *Step 2.* **Invest** *reserves into your investment vehicles.* Once you've stocked your reserves with financial fuel, it's time to pour that money into your investment vehicles.

- *Step 3.* **Convert** *investments into further investments and lifestyle cash flow.* Take profits and flow them back into your reserve vehicle to have more capital for investments. Eventually, you'll have enough cash flow to support your dream lifestyle.

Step One: Reserve

Reserve Financial Fuel

I hope this doesn't come as a surprise, but you need money for this system to work. In other words, you need to utilize a single-digit investment called your *reserve vehicle*. This is an alternative to a savings account that grows 5 to 7 percent tax-free every year while it waits to be deployed.

The entire system is rooted in your ability to set aside a reserve, invest those reserves into high-ROI vehicles, and convert the outcomes into more wealth. The good news is you've (hopefully) got a job, and you're already trading time for dollars. However, you may also be in a situation where there is no money left after paying your bills. If that is the case, it also means there is currently no financial fuel for investments.

The natural tendency is to spend 10 percent more or less than you make. This inclination is actually a derivative of *Parkinson's Law*, which states that "work expands to the time available for its completion."

We do the same thing with money that we do with time. Our budget expands to what we can afford—and often to more than we can afford.

If this is a natural instinct, then I guess it's time to fight nature. You are already making the most enormous sacrifice you will ever make (trading your valuable time for dollars). So, now I need you to commit to the following:

Save at least 20 percent of what you earn for your reserve vehicle.

I call this the *Aggressive Savings Strategy* (A.S.S.) for leveraging financial fuel into your investment vehicles. In other words, you now have a reason to move your A.S.S. to save fuel for your investments if you want your financial dreams and goals to come true.

DEVIL'S ADVOCATE

"Kris, even saving 20 percent of what I make still won't amount to much."

After a year of saving 20 percent, it may not feel like you have set enough money aside to make a difference. Here's the good news: You will be earning much higher ROIs, so you don't need to save a lot to have a significant financial impact.

"But Kris, there is no way I can save even 10 percent of what I make!"

You're not alone. According to CareerBuilder, almost 80 percent of U.S. workers live paycheck to paycheck.[18] More than 25 percent of our country has no savings at all, and 70 percent of workers making less than $100,000 are in debt. Not to mention more than half of minimum wage workers have to work more than one job to make ends meet.

I say all of that to say *yes*, it's going to be a challenge. But yes, you can do it.

ACTION STEP!   For this system to function, you must save $1 out of every $5 you earn. If you're accustomed to spending every dime, I know 20 percent seems like a huge ask.

Find a way. Rethink your finances. Look at your budget and see where you can make temporary sacrifices. If you can't do 20 percent, start with 10 percent, but then create a 90-day plan to increase your savings to 20 percent.

If you are struggling to save, you may find some reassurance in the fact that the fourth vehicle in your fleet is designed to make money on the side, so you do not have to rely solely on your day job for reserve capital. However, if 20 percent (or even just 10 percent) is still too much of a stretch, go to **KrisKrohn.com/Save** to find some smart, easy-to-implement strategies for saving more so that you can invest more.

You can be an outlier and rise to the challenge. I did it starting with *nothing*, and so can you.

Fueling your reserve is a commitment that comes with an almost immeasurable payoff!

Before I share the next two steps in my Wealth Creation System, I would like you to intentionally pause. It's time to decide how much of your hard-earned income you'll reserve as fuel for future high-ROI investments.

In reality, 20 percent should be the *minimum*. That means you may be able to save more, or you may not be able to save 20 percent yet (in which case you need a plan to get there). Decide the exact percentage you are going to set aside each month as financial fuel for your investments.

> **I am going to commit to saving _____ percent of my net monthly income to fuel my reserve.**

Make this your highest financial priority.

You need this reserve for investing like you need air for breathing.

Once you have filled the reserve with financial fuel for your investment vehicles, it's time to put that money to work through the rest of the system.

Step Two: Invest

Invest Financial Fuel into Three More Vehicles

The next step in the Wealth Creation System is to *invest*.

As you begin saving 20 percent of your income (see more in Chapter Five), your goal is to reserve enough money to fuel the next three investment vehicles (covered in Chapters Six through Eight). This step empowers your money to produce double, triple, and quadruple-digit ROIs.

The three investment vehicles include real estate and shares in specific types of companies as passive income and business as active income. These investments vary in size and will become easier to understand as you read about each one.

Step Three: Convert

Convert into More Investments and Lifestyle Cash Flow

Once you correctly implement the first two steps in the Wealth Creation System, your money will naturally lead you into step three by *converting* into two things:

1. *Cash flow.* Cash flow is money that your investments pay you back (also called profits and dividends) that can then be reinvested and/or utilized to fund your lifestyle.

2. *Increased asset value.* Your investments will become more valuable with time, so they can eventually be sold for even greater profits.

As your investments start generating cash flow, it is vital to redirect the flow back into your reserve to reinvest. More investments produce more cash flow. Allow the *cycle* to continue moving forward, and you will eventually have enough cash flow to support your dream lifestyle.

At that point, it won't even be a "cycle" of cash flow. It will become a "cyclone" of wealth.

I enthusiastically invite you to get hooked on growing your money and making it work for you. The goal is to earn an ROI that you can multiply over and over again. In a nutshell, you are putting compounding interest to work on something exciting. This starts happening at a double-digit ROI level and gets more appealing as it goes along.

Imagine earning a 25 percent ROI on a real estate deal. Then you sell that property in five years and use that profit to invest in two more properties, both of which deliver similar returns. That means the original investment is now earning a collective 50 percent ROI. If you repeat the process again in five years, you will be earning a 100 per-cent ROI.

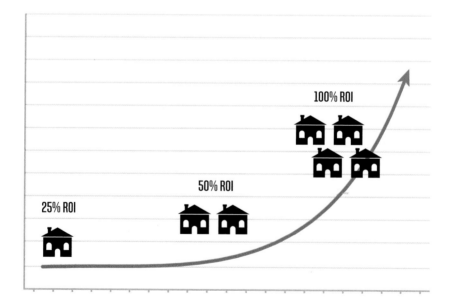

Imagine the feeling of doubling your money in 90 days. Feels good, doesn't it? Are you the kind of person who will take the spoils of war and go on a spending spree, or will you take the profit and put it back into the system to increase the gains?

Your answer to that question says a lot about how well this system will work for you. And if the idea of reinvesting that money gets you excited, then you and I have a lot in common.

Even if you start with a small investment, thanks to the power of compounding ROI, this system can create a *tsunami of results* as you reinvest. The longer the profits stay in the system, the more they multiply, and the bigger your ROI becomes. Your financial fuel (that 20 percent reserve) is what initially generates this momentum. The more you put in, the more you get back.

You should become obsessed with investing instead of spending or penny-pinching.

The more you invest, the more cash flow you generate, and the more it comes back to you. With every cyclone rotation, the money gets more significant, which means your net worth grows, which means your dreams manifest. Before you know it, you are an ultra-successful entrepreneur and philanthropist who is living your best life while preserving your most important asset, which you know by now is time.

Financial Freedom Roadmap

Combine the Compounding ROI Investment Strategy with the Three-Step Wealth Creation System, and what do you get? The Financial Freedom Roadmap. Check out how it looks visually on the next page.

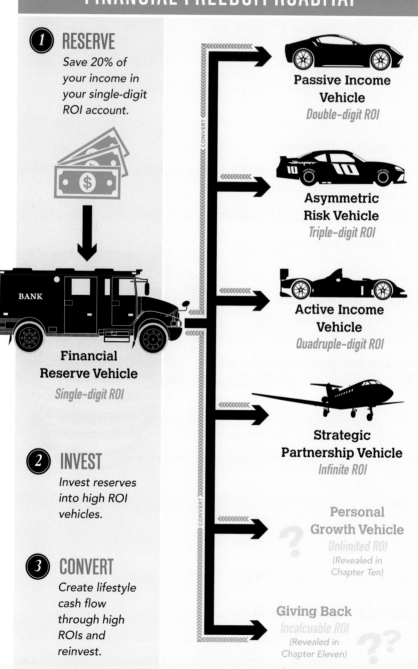

FINANCIAL FREEDOM ROADMAP

1 RESERVE
Save 20% of your income in your single-digit ROI account.

BANK

Financial Reserve Vehicle
Single-digit ROI

2 INVEST
Invest reserves into high ROI vehicles.

3 CONVERT
Create lifestyle cash flow through high ROIs and reinvest.

CONVERT

Passive Income Vehicle
Double-digit ROI

Asymmetric Risk Vehicle
Triple-digit ROI

Active Income Vehicle
Quadruple-digit ROI

Strategic Partnership Vehicle
Infinite ROI

Personal Growth Vehicle
Unlimited ROI
(Revealed in Chapter Ten)

Giving Back
Incalcuable ROI
(Revealed in Chapter Eleven)

Step 1: Reserve

Reserve money by implementing your Aggressive Savings Strategy (your A.S.S.). View this as your top financial priority. Your goal is to figure out how to save 20 percent of your paycheck every month. That money will funnel into your financial reserve vehicle that will deliver a single-digit ROI (Chapter Five).

Step 2: Invest

Invest that reserve into the next four investment vehicles. In Part Three, you'll learn about two additional investments that are not "investments" in the traditional sense but are absolutely *critical* to your success.

> **Part Three details two unconventional "investments" that you can't live without!**

Step 3: Convert

Convert these investments to produce a consistent return that you feed back into your financial reserve vehicle. Then repeat the cycle (that will soon become a *cyclone* of wealth).

This is the Financial Freedom Roadmap that includes the strategy and system to help you build wealth. In subsequent chapters, I will explain all five investment vehicles in more detail so you can harness each one's financial power. And don't miss Part Three to discover the remaining two unconventional "investments" that have changed the trajectory of my life far more than anything else.

How much financial fuel is in your tank?

Understanding how to invest money into the most well-equipped vehicles is worthless if you don't have any financial fuel for your reserve tank. Bottom line: If you don't set aside a portion of the money you earn for investments, this system will not work.

You want this system to work. You *need* this system to work.

Stop trying to assemble that IKEA coffee table without the proper pieces and without the instruction booklet. That's just a lesson in futility and frustration!

Follow the steps. Trust the system.

Accumulation Mindset vs. Residual Income Mindset

Our society promotes an *accumulation mindset*—we are told to go to work and trade time for money. Experts then tell us to "save as much as possible for retirement." You now know that the numbers prove this outdated retirement model is doomed to fail.

The goal should not be to save a certain amount of money but to empower your investments to predictably and safely produce a certain amount of *residual income*.

Well, the great news is that high-ROI investments also tend to produce a really high residual income. You may need $2.9 million or more to provide a six-figure post-retirement income with a traditional financial planner. However, you can create that same result with a lot less money by changing your goal from "save x amount of money" to "earn x in residual income."

Here are a few of the critical differences between society's limiting accumulation mindset and a millionaire's recurring income mindset.

ACCUMULATION MINDSET	RECURRING INCOME MINDSET
Scarcity	Abundance
Saves money over time	Multiplies net worth
Saves in uncollateralized vehicles	Loads up on collateralized assets
Subject to markets, inflation, taxes	Leverages control to create relative immunity
Depends on experts for financial success	Depends on self for financial success
Thinks security comes from money	Knows security comes from applied knowledge
Waits for opportunities	Creates opportunity
Thinks high returns come from high risks	Understands high returns come from mitigating risk

If you find that you relate to the mindset in the left column more than the mindset in the right, give yourself a little grace. It takes time to undo the damaging programming from our childhood. If you're anything like me, you saw your parents operate from a place of lack rather than abundance.

You can break that cycle, but it takes time, patience, and discipline!

CHAPTER FOUR CHECKPOINT

1. The Financial Freedom Roadmap is a battle-tested investment strategy and a proven three-step system.

2. My *Compounding ROI Investment Strategy* builds wealth through five vehicles: 1) Single-digit ROI from your reserve tank, 2) Double-digit ROI from passive real estate income, 3) Triple-digit ROI from passive market income, 4) Quadruple-digit ROI from business, and 5) Infinite ROI through strategic partnerships.

3. My *Three-Step Wealth Creation System* is comprised of three key action steps that work together:
1) Reserve by saving 20 percent of your income (aka your Aggressive Savings Strategy or A.S.S.),
2) Invest and earn double, triple, quadruple-digit, and infinite ROI, and 3) Convert into lifestyle cash flow and reinvestment capital.

4. The more you save, the more you can invest. The more you can invest, the more you can convert to cash flow and reinvest to create a cycle that transforms into a cyclone.

5. My Compounding ROI Investment Strategy and Three-Step Wealth Creation System combine to create my *Financial Freedom Roadmap*. You can harness this financial power to build your wealth to previously unimaginable levels.

Most folks think
they aren't good at
earning money, when
what they don't know
is how to use it.

FIVE

YOUR FINANCIAL RESERVE VEHICLE

Single-Digit ROI

EVERYBODY DISMISSES SQUIRRELS as rats with fluffy tails, but I think they're pretty clever. Aside from their cunning ability to hack any squirrel-proof bird feeder known to man, they are also excellent planners.

You can bet there are no foolish squirrels out there eating every single bite of food they worked so hard to collect. And if there were, those squirrels wouldn't even be around long enough to tell the harrowing tale of the winter they almost didn't make it.

No, they're smarter than that. Squirrels instinctively know that they need their reserves to be *overflowing* by the time winter comes around. So, they work hard to collect more than they need to eat in the present to save for the future.

I bet you never thought you'd be reading this, but you need to be more like a squirrel.

You must set one acorn aside into the "knothole" known as your reserve vehicle for every five acorns you collect. Logically, I call this investment vehicle your *armored truck*. Utilizing a savings vehicle with a built-in ROI is intelligent and also an indispensable first step in my roadmap.

Skip this vehicle, and your quest to have it all will stop right here, right now. I assume that doesn't sound good to you, so I invite you to read about this reserve vehicle with an open mind and the curious nature of a squirrel.

Curiosity will take you far in life. The curious people in this world are the ones who create opportunities and who see closed doors as challenges waiting to be conquered. So, dig up some curiosity and put it to work as we continue.

Meet Your Armored Truck

There's no denying it: Money is what makes more money.

In chemistry, the *law of conservation of mass* states that matter cannot be created or destroyed, but it can change forms. An easy way to explain this concept is to imagine a wax candle with a wick. Once you light the candle and it burns down, it looks like the wax is gone. What really happened is that the resin has been transformed into *gases* (water vapor and carbon dioxide). But in reality, no matter (and therefore no mass) is lost through the process of burning.

> *"What are you doing to me, Kris? First, you make me do math, and now you are giving me a chemistry lesson?"*

Hey, don't blame me! Your teachers told you all along that what you were learning would be helpful later. Here is the bottom line and why I bring all of this up ...

As great as it would be, there is no way to manifest money out of thin air—that is, unless you're the government. Eventually, however, their money-printing schemes will backfire in a big way (you can't defy the laws of nature and not answer for it).

About the closest a human being can get to "manifesting money out of thin air" is utilizing the infinite ROI vehicle we'll cover in Chapter Nine. But even then, the money still has to be stored up by someone in order to be available to you.

So, yes, it takes money to make money. Where the finesse comes into play is how you set up money to attract *more money* to it. This chapter is all about that finesse.

You need a reserve earning a single-digit ROI set aside to create peace of mind but, more importantly, to invest in higher-ROI opportunities.

What you need is that armored truck that stores all of the fuel that will be used to power up the rest of the investments. On our Financial Freedom Roadmap, it's destination number one!

Your Aggressive Savings Strategy (A.S.S.) is that magic savings number we've already discussed. This monthly 20 percent comprises the

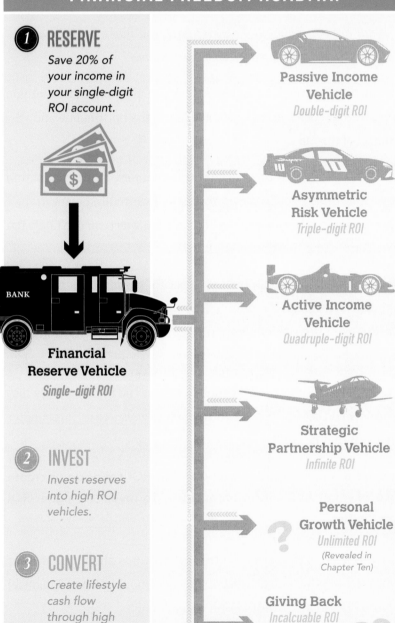

FINANCIAL FREEDOM ROADMAP

① RESERVE
Save 20% of your income in your single-digit ROI account.

Financial Reserve Vehicle
Single-digit ROI

② INVEST
Invest reserves into high ROI vehicles.

③ CONVERT
Create lifestyle cash flow through high ROIs and reinvest.

BANK

Passive Income Vehicle
Double-digit ROI

Asymmetric Risk Vehicle
Triple-digit ROI

Active Income Vehicle
Quadruple-digit ROI

Strategic Partnership Vehicle
Infinite ROI

Personal Growth Vehicle
Unlimited ROI
(Revealed in Chapter Ten)

Giving Back
Incalcuable ROI
(Revealed in Chapter Eleven)

funds you must stash into your armored truck. Now, you *could* place it into a savings account, but that would earn less than 1 percent ROI with no additional benefits.

But there is a more innovative way.

Years ago, when I started having success with my new investments, my reserves began to grow right along with my investment philosophy. Eventually, I had six figures just sitting around, collecting dust in a savings account. Seeing that balance inertly staring at me, doing nothing, got me wondering.

What do the wealthy do with their large cash reserves?

We know they don't have savings accounts at their local banks with a few million bucks in there. So, what happens to their excess capital? I began interviewing millionaires and billionaires to unearth the answer to this question and others.

First, I discovered that making a lot of money causes an almost instantaneous and unquenchable desire to find the most tax shelters possible. With *big* money comes the *big* responsibility to be intelligent and save for other lucrative investments.

The second thing I discovered is a specific type of savings vehicle that many businessmen and women seem to favor. To my surprise, they stash cash in an underutilized kind of life insurance policy that provides numerous *living* benefits.

Wait—life insurance policies are only payable on death, right?

It turns out that is not always true. Yet, for some reason, this strategy gets overlooked and even ridiculed in traditional financial investment circles. *For the life of me, I can't figure out why this is the case.*

I finally determined it must result from a combination of cognitive dissonance and a limited mindset. Because once you start using a life policy for savings, I assure you there is nothing laughable about it.

Now, let me be crystal clear:

I couldn't care less about life insurance as an investment based on the *death* benefit.

In fact, I'm opposed to it (a topic for another time). Life insurance is traditionally about investing in a death benefit for your heirs. However, I'm talking about life insurance policies with *living* benefits.

To my surprise, a number of my millionaire friends didn't know about these policies either. This is probably because most life insurance agents don't even know about them! Those who *do* know about them keep their mouths shut. Why? Sadly, it's because insurance companies will cut commissions by up to 90 percent when these policies are created.

Self-interest is a heck of a thing, isn't it?

If you're feeling skeptical, I get it. Fortunately, it's true—you can earn an extra 5 to 7 percent ROI on your investments just by using this particular kind of life insurance savings account. As a bonus, this policy also provides a death benefit and protection from inflation and lawsuits (in some states only).

That's what a cash value dividend-paying life insurance policy (or CVDP) is all about.

I call it your "life insurance savings account."

I use it just like a bank account because it gives me a whole slew of perks that traditional bank accounts do not. Here are the top seven benefits you'll be most interested in discovering.

1. Guarantees an ROI.

By having your cash tucked away in this life insurance savings account, you will receive a certain percent ROI guaranteed by state law (actual rate will vary by carrier and generally range from 2 percent to 3.75 percent). I love this guaranteed percent because every year, inflation drives the dollar's value down by approximately 2 to 3 percent. This ROI hedges against inflation while your money waits to be used for the next investment.

2. Pays you dividends.

Most insurance companies pay an additional 1 to 3 percent annual dividend on some whole life policies. In many ways, these dividends are similar to traditional investment dividends, representing a share of a public company's profit. Your dividend amount depends on the amount you pay into the policy. For example:

A $50,000 policy that offers a 3 percent dividend will pay you, the policyholder, $1,500 annually ($50,000 x .03 = $1,500).

Then, let's say you contribute another $2,000 in premium the following year. The policy will pay a 3 percent dividend on that as well. So, doing the math, that comes to $60 dollars ($2,000 additional premium x .03 = $60).

Add those together, and that means you will receive a total of $1,560 next year ($1,500 + $60 = $1,560).

Imagine increasing your pile of money and then getting paid 3 percent on that increase every time you do. These amounts can increase over time to levels that *more than offset* some costs associated with the premium payments!

These dividends are not guaranteed, but if you add their potential to the guaranteed percent, it means you can produce up to a 5 to7 percent annual ROI. Remember, a single-ROI savings account of any kind will not make you wealthy. However, it *can* counter the effects of inflation and cover the cost of borrowing against the policy.

If you had the choice to earn up to 7 percent ROI on your insurance savings account or a 0.1 percent ROI on your local savings account, which one would you choose? It's just common sense (which doesn't seem to be quite as common anymore).

3. Allows you to borrow cash value to buy more assets.

This is my favorite part! You can pull reserves out of your life insurance savings account and put them into other investment vehicles.

This is called *borrowing against the cash value* of your policy.

It enables you to take your money out and still earn money as if it's sitting in your life insurance savings account. You're actually making money in two places at once, which is an incredible example of leverage. The same cannot be said for traditional savings. Once you take money out of a conventional bank, all of the meager benefits stop right there.

IMAGINE THE POSSIBILITIES OF COMPOUNDING ROI

Let's assume you are earning a 2 percent ROI, plus a 4 percent dividend, for a total of 6 percent. Then, you take money out of your policy to fund an investment property that produces 25 percent annual ROI.

You might be thinking, "What's the cost of borrowing money out of my policy?"

Currently, you can borrow that money for as low as 3 percent, while you are simultaneously earning that 6 percent. Translation: even after you take that money out for the real estate transaction, you could still be earning a net 3 percent on your life insurance policy while the money is sitting in your other investment earning 25 percent for a total ROI of now 28 percent!

That is the power of compounding ROI and a true example of leverage in action! In case you've ever wondered how the wealthy grow their money—well, this is how.

4. Enables tax-free growth.

As you start earning more money, it becomes increasingly important to minimize your taxable income. The guaranteed percent ROI and the 1 to 3 percent dividends all grow tax-free. The more money you make and the more your investments grow, the more critical this benefit becomes.

5. Offers guaranteed protection (varies by state).

The government views a person's life insurance as a different type of protected asset class. It means that, currently, any cash value held in an insurance policy is not litigable in some states (always check with your specific state's rules and regulations first, as protection varies by state). If someone tries to attack you legally, in certain states they can't touch this life insurance savings account. In this way, your insurance policies become an integral and immutable part of your legacy.

6. Provides a death benefit.

Like any other type of life insurance policy, the CVDP life insurance policy contains a death benefit. There is comfort in knowing that if I make a premature or unplanned exit from the earth, I will be leaving my family with a large sum of generally tax-free money. Beyond that, I am also insured for a large enough death benefit to cover any outstanding liabilities or debts.

Make a plan that leaves your loved ones with assets and a way to eliminate liabilities.

Later, I will show you how to acquire real estate, how to invest in the market, and how to build businesses, all in a way that utilizes leverage. I love putting other people's money to work, and I know you will, too. But this also means you will have some "good debts" that are making you money. So, should you die prematurely, this death benefit gives your beneficiaries a way to pay off those good debts, ensuring you leave loved ones with a pile of assets instead of a giant liability headache.

7. Delivers disability protection (for an additional cost).

Suppose you ever become mentally or physically disabled. In that case, the insurance carrier covers those costs and continues paying for the rest of your policy. It's a valuable benefit that you may choose to add to your policy.

I store my savings in a life insurance policy because I continue earning dividends and interest even when I borrow the money and put it into my investments.

This reserve vehicle, my own Loomis truck, supercharges my double-digit, triple-digit, and quadruple-digit ROIs and provides the benefits mentioned above.

Utilizing a life insurance savings account makes sense. Who wouldn't want to earn an extra 2 to 3 percent or more on top of their existing investments?

DEVIL'S ADVOCATE

"I don't know, Kris, this sounds too good to be true. What's the catch?"

There is no catch. There is only a lack of information. In truth, large insurance companies are a lot like banks. Many of them have been around for over 150 years, and most of them have never missed a dividend payment. These are not fly-by-night operations. We're talking about large, protected institutions with guaranteed products that have been around for over a century.

How to Leverage Your Armored Truck

Now that you've learned more about your new intelligent single-digit ROI reserve vehicle, let's talk about how to intelligently leverage it. Like I stated earlier, you stash cash in a smart single-digit ROI vehicle for two reasons:

Reason 1:
To reserve financial fuel for future investments.

You now know that the law of conservation of mass proves you can't manifest money out of thin air. And unless you're David Copperfield or Houdini, you are going to need more than magic. Aggressively saving at least 20 percent of your current active income is what quickly meets the needs of your double-digit to infinite ROI opportunities.

That makes setting 20 percent aside for higher ROI investment vehicles your top priority. The *most* crucial factor in whether you become financially free comes down to your discipline in setting money aside for these investments. I repeat this because it's too important to miss.

Reason 2:

To reserve financial fuel for your S.W.A.N. Account.

Can you remember a time when you were constantly checking your bank account to make sure your balance could cover your upcoming bills? Have you ever woken up to the sinking feeling of seeing a negative balance and an overdraft notification?

These moments create extreme financial stress, and that's the last thing you need when shifting your focus to investing. Your reserve vehicle is more than just a place to "stash cash" for investments. It's a way to create a reserve that allows you to sleep at night. Here's an important question:

"What is the minimum amount of money you need in an emergency fund that will enable you to sleep well at night?"

Determine what that amount is, write it down, and then work to make it happen. I called this your S.W.A.N. account, or your "Sleep Well At Night" account. Your first goal should be to save that figure and stash it in your life insurance savings account. There are three different S.W.A.N. savings levels that can help determine how to proceed with your investments. If you'd like to learn more about the three levels and how much to invest in each, go to **KrisKrohn.com/SWAN**.

According to CNBC, the majority (67 percent) of Americans save less than 10 percent of their income.[19] And according to Yahoo! Finance, almost half of the American workforce invests *none* of their money.[20]

None.

These folks are not building any kind of a future where freedom or confidence exists. They are in survival mode, living paycheck to paycheck. Don't be a cautionary tale for your children. You can do better for them and for you.

YOUR RESERVE VEHICLE IN ACTION

RESERVE: Set at least 20 percent aside in your life insurance savings account to build up an adequate S.W.A.N. account and higher ROI investment vehicles.

INVEST: Borrow money from your life insurance savings account to make your next investment.

CONVERT: Deposit earnings back into your reserve vehicle to build up for your next investment.

This process becomes exponentially more exciting every time you add new investments to your portfolio, and your earnings experience the same exponential growth.

Picture, for a moment, those little toy push cars you may have played with as a child. You know the kind I'm talking about—they require a little bit of force to get them moving. But once you get those wheels turning and let them go, they zoom off with incredible speed.

You may not know those tiny cars are powered by a friction motor operated by a flywheel. A *flywheel* is a wheel rotating on a shaft. Its momentum gives almost uniform rotational speed to all connected machinery.

Flywheels are used to provide continuous power output in systems where the energy source is not constant. With a flywheel, once in motion, each rotation requires less momentum and spins faster.

Now picture that concept (a "money flywheel") driving your wealth.

On its own, your 20 percent savings is just a static number that provides the ability to sleep well at night. But put it into the machine and give it a push, and your investments start producing more profits.

Each time you put those back into your reserve vehicle and into more investments, this speeds up the process again and adds more momentum. Add to this the momentum you gain by restoring your time, growing your assets, increasing your cash flow, and achieving your goals.

And this, my friends, is how you reach financial freedom.

Life is all about momentum and energy, and your money works according to the same principles.

YOUR MONEY FLYWHEEL POWERS YOUR FINANCIAL CYCLONE

At this point, I hope you're as excited as I was when I started learning about life insurance saving accounts. Many people I talk to about these accounts have the same questions, so I created a case study with an accompanying FAQs section on life insurance savings accounts that you can find at **KrisKrohn.com/CaseStudy**.

How to Add an Armored Truck to the Fleet

Rob Gill is my life insurance company business partner and an authority on using life insurance to fuel your investments. When it comes to using a life insurance savings account, here is what he tells his clients:

> *"Buying and selling property by 'borrowing' from a life insurance savings account is the best way to offset inflation at the same time you establish cash flow. This method achieves the best results on the most accelerated timeline. Never pass on a great real estate opportunity because you don't have the ability to quickly access a pile of money."*

Rob further agrees that reserving your financial fuel and then pumping that fuel into investment like real estate is a great way to build wealth. And you can quickly pay back the down payment borrowed from your reserve vehicle with the cash flow generated from other investments.

You are paying yourself back with interest. It's brilliant.

This is not something you can set up yourself. You have to go through a licensed agent. Remember when I told you that your financial advisor won't want you to read this book? That is because the vast majority of advisors are not well-informed on these types of policies.

That means it's decision time. Are you going to take action and find answers, or are you going to stay stuck on the sidelines?

Once you have decided what amount of money you can save (could be more or less than 20 percent for now), the second action is to visit the link below and set up your life insurance savings account for free.

Over the years, I've met with insurance agents and carriers and interviewed them on best practices for setting up a functional and maximized life insurance savings account. I'm sad to share that many insurance agencies are not up to the task, either due to a lack of understanding or experience. Fortunately, I've come across a few organizations that I trust to put these policies together correctly.

Remember, there's a reason why the wealthy don't put their money in regular bank accounts. A life insurance savings account protects your money, maximizes your tax benefits AND doubles your earning potential. For a complimentary Cash Flow Analysis (that saves the average person $9,000), and to learn more about getting set up with a life insurance savings account, visit this link: **KrisKrohn.com/CashFlow**.

When you contact agents that I have already vetted and approved, you can be confident that they: 1) understand this vehicle, 2) can expertly help you set it up, and 3) will show you how to utilize it.

Now that you understand the importance of setting up an intelligent, single-digit ROI investment in the form of your life insurance savings account, we can shift to an even more exciting topic—higher ROIs!

Put 20 percent of your income into a reserve vehicle and convert it into double-digit ROIs. This alone will enable you to create 27 times more wealth than society's retirement vehicles create. That's all it takes to win, and yet we will discuss even more significant gains later in the book.

Over the next four chapters, you will feel the *need for speed* as I show you how to accelerate the process through double-digit, triple-digit, quadruple-digit, and infinite ROIs. So, buckle up as you prepare to invest in your new high-performance vehicles. These vehicles will enable you to have it all!

CHAPTER FIVE CHECKPOINT

1. You must save to invest in order to produce double-digit ROIs or higher. There's no getting around this step.

2. After years of interviewing the world's wealthiest people, I discovered they use a different form of savings than the rest of us—a *cash value dividend-paying life insurance policy* that I call a life insurance savings account.

3. A few of the potential benefits of using an insurance policy as your savings account include guaranteed percent ROI, dividends up to 3 percent, tax-free growth, protected money, and both life and death benefits.

4. There are two underlying reasons why setting up a reserve vehicle is the first step in my roadmap: to allow for larger-ROI investments and to create a S.W.A.N. account.

5. Treating your reserves and cash flows this way creates a flywheel effect that leverages momentum to exponentially grow your money.

6. Traditional financial advisors may not be well versed in this investment vehicle. Utilize my list of vetted professionals who can help you add an armored truck to your financial fleet.

The best investment
on earth is earth.

LOUIS GLICKMAN

SIX

YOUR PASSIVE INCOME VEHICLE

Double-Digit ROI

MOST PEOPLE DON'T HAVE IT IN THEM to buck the system. By and large, we are a nation of people who will follow the rules and do what we're told. I certainly didn't question the conclusion that college and a full-time desk job was the path to happiness (or at least to adulthood).

I just did what I was expected to do.

Society and my dad told me to get a degree, so that's what I was faithfully doing. The rules also said I needed to get a job that may or may not be torture. Did it matter if I hated it? Heck no! What was important was that it provided a stable paycheck and maybe health benefits.

> *"I'll just keep my head down, and in 40 or so years, there is a chance I'll have enough to retire as long as I don't live too long after that!"*

Then I met three extraordinary people.

Let's call them Bill, Bob, and Beth.

Bill, Bob, and Beth had fancy stuff. They lived in nice houses, and they drove expensive cars. I was in awe and could hardly imagine what it must be like to have possessions other people admired. (At the time, I drove a 1993 Subaru Justy. Google it for a good laugh.)

But here's the real kicker: Bill, Bob, and Beth also seemed to be getting the most out of their most valuable asset. *It looked like they had all the time in the world!*

If Bill felt like spending a day on the lake, he loaded up his boat and went out on the water. If Bob wanted to spend the day riding his Harley, he grabbed his helmet and fired up the hog. If Beth wanted to have a girls' lunch and spend the rest of the afternoon at the spa with her closest friends, she made a few phone calls and was on her way.

What did these folks have in common besides enjoying every day to its fullest?

At the time, Bill, Bob, and Beth had each made over $10 million in real estate, which afforded them the flexibility and opportunity to enjoy such extraordinary lifestyles.

Were they just lucky, or could anyone experience that same success? I wasn't sure, but I was ready to find out—and that's how I first caught the real estate bug.

I've Got a Fever (and the Only Prescription is More Real Estate)

When I met these successful real estate heavy hitters, I was making a scant $18,700 a year working a full-time job that I *loathed*. But I had also started formulating my roadmap and had worked diligently to amass $5,000 in savings (even though I didn't have a life insurance savings account yet).

Reserve in hand, I went hunting for my first property. With a mentor's guidance, I bought a home valued at $150,000 for just $110,000. I closed on the house, wholly consumed with feelings of terror, excitement, and pride. I invested less than $4,000 (a 3 percent down payment, which is still common today) and was officially the newest player in the real estate game.

Instantly, that $4,000 increased my net worth to $40,000, a ten-fold return. I went from a negative to a positive net worth with a few strokes of the pen.

What an exhilarating feeling!

Even better, I rented out the basement of our new home for $550 a month, which covered the entire mortgage. My wife and I were now living "rent-free" with our monthly mortgage payment completely paid for by our basement dwellers. The excitement of it all encouraged me to want to do it again. And again. And then again after that.

DEVIL'S ADVOCATE

"You got lucky, Kris. Try doing that in today's economy!"

Sorry, but that's just an excuse (and not a very original one). I have thousands of students following this exact strategy today. It worked then, and it works now.

Twelve months after my first purchase, I got an $18,900 home equity line of credit (HELOC) on the property. If you aren't familiar with a HELOC, it's like a credit card tied to your home's equity. Because it's a *secured loan* (a loan in which you pledge some asset as collateral), the interest rate is substantially lower than those associated with unsecured debt like traditional credit cards.

I used this credit line to buy my next house through a bank foreclosure worth over $210,000 that I acquired for just $150,000. The monthly mortgage payment on my new property would be $1,000.

I decided to do a rent-to-own, or *lease option*, based on another mentor's advice. I found a family willing to pay $3,000 as a down payment (common with a lease option) and then $1,600 a month in rent. This amount was $300 higher than it would have been with a traditional rental.

WHAT IS A LEASE OPTION?

When I purchased my second property, I offered it as a rent-to-own, or lease option, based on one of my mentor's recommendations. This is leasing a home with an option for the tenant to buy it. One of the most obvious benefits of this option is you can collect a higher monthly rent than with traditional rentals (in the example above with my first lease option, I earned $300 more than I would have with a straightforward rental agreement).

My mentor explained that this strategy, compared to a straightforward rental, can be twice as profitable while creating a valuable benefit for the investment home's family. Your tenants can work toward buying the house rather than just renting it.

I used this lease option strategy with my first 25 homes, and it provided over $12,000 a month in residual income. This cash flow allowed me to quit my job, multiply my portfolio, create greater cash flow from high-ROI investments, and live the good life. I wrote a book documenting this entire DIY strategy called, *The Strait Path to Real Estate Wealth.*

VISIT KRISKROHN.COM/BOOK TO GRAB A FREE COPY.

Just like that, I was making an additional $600 every single month ($1,600 rent less my $1,000 mortgage payment).

Add the $600 cash flow to the $550 we collected each month from renting out our basement, and I felt pretty darn good about the investments I was making. Not to mention, my total net worth was now over $100,000 between the two properties.

My monthly income from my full-time job was just over $1,500. Without taking on a second job or working double shifts, I had just added $1,150 to my bottom line every month.

After just two real estate transactions, my monthly income increased by close to 75 percent but required virtually no additional time. Needless to say, I was hooked.

My wife came to me one day for a bit of clarification. "Hey, Kris, I'm not sure where this extra $600 belongs on our budget spreadsheet."

I thought for a minute. "I guess we need to create a new job income line called 'real estate income.' What have we been doing with the $550 rent?"

Kalenn responded, "I've been aggressively paying down our debt."

"It's probably a good idea for us to create two extra line items in the income category."

I was totally caught off guard when she then asked with a smile, "So, when can we buy our next house?"

A new property meant hundreds of extra passive dollars each month to help us get out of debt more quickly. Kalenn wanted more—and so did I.

I'll never forget how elating it felt working as a team to create an aggressive plan for achieving our financial freedom. We decided that with a $10,000 residual income each month, I would no longer need to work a traditional job. To meet that goal, I needed around 20 properties, with each of them producing $500 a month.

Here is the simple math it took to figure that out:

Passive income needed: $10,000

Average income per house: $500

$10,000 / $500 =
20 rental homes needed to reach our goal

I had specific income and time goals, and now I knew what it would take to achieve them.

DEVIL'S ADVOCATE

"But Kris, I'll never be able to get my spouse/partner on board."

Spouses offer that all-important stabilizing opinion. Their perspectives can keep you from either being too aggressive or too conservative. Just remember that you may have decided to invest because you gained the knowledge it takes to have *confidence* in your decision.

Respect your spouse by offering them the same—give them the gift of knowledge by helping them understand the *why* behind your plan.

Come to them with real numbers and reasonable expectations (don't be "pie in the sky" about it because that will lead to disappointment and an erosion of trust).

I wanted my wife's support, and I eventually got it. She was terrified at first, but after the first two homes, she felt more confident in me and the plan. In the beginning, I asked her to trust me and take a leap. Still, I would have made the real estate decisions I did with or without her confidence. I had simply determined it was the best way to fulfill my promises to her.

I took a risk, but I did so intelligently. And I wasn't alone. I had mentors who guided me. Having a subject matter expert with a proven track record watching diligently makes up the difference for what you may lack. Gain the knowledge you need, enlist the help of the right mentors, and that is how you simultaneously honor your partner and your goals.

The Science and Speed of Real Estate Investing

In case it isn't obvious, what we've been talking about so far is the next step in the Financial Freedom Roadmap. It's the second vehicle in the fleet—your **double-digit ROI sports car**.

Let's review our roadmap and where real estate fits on the path to financial freedom.

As you'll learn in this chapter, cash flow from real estate becomes passive income that you can use to re-invest or fund your lifestyle. When executed properly, it can consistently and predictably provide you with solid double-digit ROIs.

This sports car was the original investment vehicle that enabled me to ride on the fast-track to wealth accumulation at a young age. I went to work finding 20 properties that would produce at least $500 a month in cash flow, and within a few years, I said goodbye to the cubicle life forever.

FINANCIAL FREEDOM ROADMAP

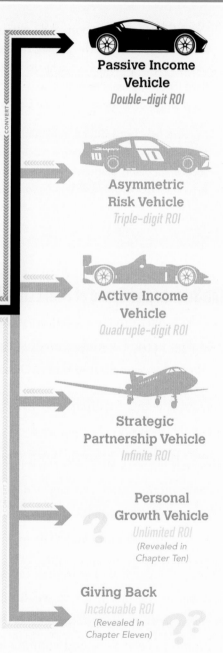

1 RESERVE

Save 20% of your income in your single-digit ROI account.

Financial Reserve Vehicle

Single-digit ROI

Passive Income Vehicle

Double-digit ROI

Asymmetric Risk Vehicle

Triple-digit ROI

Active Income Vehicle

Quadruple-digit ROI

Strategic Partnership Vehicle

Infinite ROI

2 INVEST

Invest reserves into high ROI vehicles.

Personal Growth Vehicle

Unlimited ROI

(Revealed in Chapter Ten)

3 CONVERT

Create lifestyle cash flow through high ROIs and reinvest.

Giving Back

Incalcuable ROI

(Revealed in Chapter Eleven)

I became financially free using this double-digit ROI vehicle, and we haven't even gotten to triple-digit ROIs and beyond!

Real estate has the *potential* to be a robust wealth foundation as long as you leverage it correctly. This vehicle allows you to put money down and sit back and watch it generate a cash flow, when done correctly.

One of the keywords I don't want you to miss is "potential."

> **POTENTIAL (ADJ, NOUN):**
> The inherent ability or capacity for growth, development, or future success that has not yet been reached.

Going back to science again (roll your eyes if needed), let's talk about potential energy in physics. *Potential energy* is the stored energy an object has because of its position or state. A few examples are a bicycle on a hill, a person at the top of the stairs, and a coiled-up spring not yet released. These are all things that have what it takes to exhibit great power and/or movement but haven't used that potential yet.

This kind of energy is often contrasted by *kinetic energy*. Potential energy is stored energy, while kinetic energy is the energy of motion or doing. When potential energy is used, it is then converted into kinetic energy. You can think of potential energy as kinetic energy waiting to happen.

When it comes to your wealth roadmap, the "potential energy" of your plan is represented by two things:

1. The accumulation of *savings* in that single-digit ROI vehicle.

2. The proper *knowledge* required to earn sizable ROIs (or in other words, knowing where to invest your money).

Without the proper knowledge, the "potential energy" found in your reserves will be wasted.

Almost every person I talk to easily understands the idea that it takes money to make money. However, the critical ingredient most miss in the potential energy equation is the *proper knowledge* aspect. Instead, most people lose their potential by allowing their misguided fears (based on lack of information) to rob them of their momentum.

Suppose you are mistrustful of real estate investing because of horror stories you've heard or hesitations you have about market fluctuations. If that's the case, I understand because I've heard and felt them, too.

But while investing in real estate can be intimidating, most people don't fail because of the market or a "bad deal." They fail because they are missing that essential ingredient—the proper knowledge.

The absolute fastest way to gain the knowledge you need is by partnering with a mentor who has made *all* the mistakes. As a result, he or she figured out the most direct path to investing success.

Why would anyone want to reinvent the real estate investing wheel? Find the right mentor who can walk you through it all properly. Shorten the time horizon by leveraging the knowledge of others!

That is why I'm here. I will remove the guesswork and provide the knowledge you need. This isn't magic or luck. There is a precision and a *science* to it, just as there is with every other consistent and reliable income-producing endeavor on the planet.

DEVIL'S ADVOCATE

"Listen, Kris, I'm not interested in becoming a landlord. Taking calls from frustrated tenants and chasing after my rent sounds like a nightmare. I'm not signing up for late-night trips to the hardware store because a tenant's toilet sprung a leak."

This is not a plan for becoming a full-time landlord. It's really about using the strategy that takes the least time, effort, and risk while producing the most profit. Later in the chapter, we'll discuss two different ways to invest. Relax in the knowledge that not all real estate paths lead to The Home Depot.

To further help you understand how to leverage real estate as a means of guaranteeing financial freedom, it's time to cover three critical components to your real estate knowledge base: 1) the seven most dynamic benefits of investing in real estate, 2) the six criteria for property selection, and 3) the number one strategy for building a passive portfolio.

Potential Energy Ingredient #1
The Seven Benefits of Real Estate Investing

Most people don't understand just how profitable real estate can be, and I get it. On the surface, making multiple five- and six-figure purchases on mostly borrowed money can be more than a little intimidating.

The good news is there are seven specific benefits of investing in real estate that make the decision to invest the obvious choice. If you leverage these benefits, you will consistently produce double-digit ROIs and make as much passive income as your heart desires.

Let's do a quick dive into each benefit and see them in action.

1. Appreciation
Owning a Rapidly Growing Tangible Asset

The amount of land that exists today on Earth is the same amount of land that will exist tomorrow. There is no way to create more land (they *did* build islands from scratch in the shape of a palm tree off the coast of Dubai, but that is a wild and crazy exception, not the rule).

As a result of the fixed nature of land, property value increases over time. More people vying for the same amount of land means higher values, year after year. And, just by owning a home, it appreciates by an average of 4.68 percent every year.

> ### APPRECIATION IN ACTION:
>
> Let's say you buy a $200,000 home in a market that is appreciating at 5 percent a year. That 5 percent is equivalent to $10,000 a year, and that increase will continue to compound year after year. With simple interest alone, that same home will be worth $250,000 after five years. Your net worth will have increased by $50,000 just by owning it.
>
> Now, imagine having 20 houses of the same value. In five years, your net worth will have increased by $1 million.

2. Cash Flow
Building a Powerful Residual Income

The *cash flow* from real estate represents the amount of money left after paying all your bills from collected rent. If you purchase property correctly, there should *always* be leftover money. I call this cash flow your "freedom dollars" because the more you accumulate, the less you need to work for your money. Your money starts working for you.

CASH FLOW IN ACTION:

If you buy a home and rent it for $1,500 a month, but your mortgage and expenses are only $1,100 a month, you are generating a $400 monthly cash flow in the form of residual income.

3. Leverage Control
Earning High ROI with the Bank's Money

Producing high ROIs in real estate is possible because of the leverage banks provide. If you have $50,000 in cash, you can only buy $50,000 worth of stocks. There is *zero* leverage in that transaction. However, with real estate, $50,000 in cash can purchase $250,000 worth of real estate. That's because banks allow you to leverage, on average, $5 for every $1 you invest. Your returns are five times greater because of the leverage!

This leverage is a critical part of how we get to a minimum 25 percent ROI through real estate investing.

LEVERAGE CONTROL IN ACTION:

A great deal on a single-family home in a good cash flow area hits the market at $200,000. The bank requires a 20 percent down payment of $40,000 to buy this home. If the home increases 10 percent in value, it is now worth $220,000. That $20,000 increase came from a $40,000 investment. In this illustration, that's a 50 percent ROI on this benefit alone.

4. Tax Benefits
Writing Off and Deferring Capital Gains

Can you imagine earning an income but paying no taxes on that income? That's what happens when you purchase real estate the right way. You are legally allowed to depreciate an asset over 27.5 years, which produces massive tax write-offs. Typically, this write-off cancels out all taxes on the positive cash flow you earned that year, with additional write-offs remaining. Even though you're show-ing a positive cash flow, the depreciation and interest expenses can-cel that income!

The end result is you have more money in your pocket, but you don't owe *any* of that money to the government. The wealthy understand this benefit and therefore work to max out their real estate holdings.

TAX BENEFITS IN ACTION:

You earned $5,000 in positive cash flow in a single year on a rental worth $220,000. The U.S. government allows you to write off that $220,000 over 27.5 years, which comes to $8,000 per year ($220,000 ÷ 27.5 years = $8,000).

The $8,000 write-off first cancels out the $5,000 you collected as a positive cash flow, with $3,000 in depreciation write-off left over ($8,000 - $5,000 = $3,000) to lower your other income. This allows you to pay even less in taxes.

So, you pocket $5,000 tax-free, and you don't have to pay taxes on another $3,000 you made elsewhere. You are getting wealth-ier with cash in hand while enjoying extra tax write-offs.

GOOD TO KNOW
DEPRECIATION

When you buy a computer, the IRS determines that it will wear out in five years, so they let you take the entire cost of the computer and write off a 20 percent (one-fifth) of the cost for each of the five years. Well, the IRS determined that most parts in a house need to be replaced within 27.5 years—so they let you take the total cost of the property and write off a twenty-seventh of it each year.

5. Market Resilience
Earning High ROIs Across Market Conditions

Real estate comes in all shapes and sizes, ranging from single-family homes to apartments, commercial real estate, raw land, and more. Most real estate sectors see their value negatively impacted during a recession. However, entry-level, single-family homes priced below the national median (more on this type of property a little later in Potential Energy Ingredient #3) are the most recession-proof type of real estate.

MARKET RESILIENCE IN ACTION:

Take a look at the projected potential decrease in home values during a recession. The most expensive homes lose a significant amount of their value (as much as 50 percent), while homes below the median lose notably less (a $200,000 home loses 9 percent by comparison). This demonstrates why properties at or below median value allow for the most remarkable market resilience:

- A $1,000,000 home can decrease to $500,000 in value.

- A $500,000 home can decrease to $300,000 in value.

- A $300,000 home can decrease to $200,000 in value.

- A $200,000 home can decrease to $180,000 in value.

- A $180,000 home can decrease to $170,000 in value.

If you purchase real estate below the median, you insulate yourself from steep market price drops. You continue to hold this property during the down economy while still earning income in the form of rent. With homes going back to the bank during recessions, rentals become even more popular during recessions, and rent prices on entry-level homes increase an average of $50 to $100 per month.

So, when a recession hits, you can buy more single-family real estate at better prices, with lower interest rates, while cashing in on higher cash flows.

GOOD TO KNOW
ARE RECESSIONS HARMFUL TO REAL ESTATE?

In a few words? *Not as much as you'd think.* On average, real estate values only diminish in two out of every five recessions.

Translation: Just because the stock market takes a hit doesn't mean real estate will. Real estate prices decrease almost exclusively when there is too much supply of homes and not enough demand for purchase. This causes a "bubble burst" of inventory and inflated prices, leading to a correction.

Another factor that helps protect real estate is the fact that investors buy property differently than the average homeowner. Investor property purchases are *countercyclical*. When everyone else is buying, they are selling, and when everyone is selling, they are buying.

During a recession, fear is at an all-time high, and consumer confidence is ultra-low, which leads people to sell their real estate at the wrong time for the wrong reasons. After the 2008 real estate crisis, I made my investors over $100 million in profits because we were buying when everyone was selling. Others were terrified to even enter the game during that time, but my strategy enabled me and my team to remain calm and increase profits.

When it comes to real estate, timing can be the difference between a massive ROI and no ROI. For more on the best time to buy real estate, check out "The Two Best Times to Buy Real Estate" at KrisKrohn.com/Timing.

6. Passive Investment
Reclaiming Your Time to Live Your Ideal Life

Besides compounding interest (the thing that made me fall in love with real estate), my other favorite part about real estate investing is that it's passive as long as you pick the proper strategy. In other words, you don't *need* to be a landlord, take midnight phone calls, or even talk to tenants unless you *want* to do those things. Some investors want that, but I certainly never did.

You can outsource nearly every part of real estate ownership. All you are left with is cash flow and the maximum return on your most valuable asset (you know by now I'm talking about your *time*).

PASSIVE INVESTMENT IN ACTION:

Real estate investment companies exist to make real estate investing passive and turnkey. After researching your best options, you select a company with a track record for having facilitated thousands of high-ROI deals in the best markets. They help you acquire properties earning double-digit ROI by:

- *Acquisition*—Researching, finding, and vetting the best deals.

- *Purchase*—Lining up financing with the top investment banks.

- *Rehab*—Coordinating any and all property repairs.

- *Property Management*—Selecting vetted tenants and managing the day-to-day process.

- *Exit Strategy*—Assisting in selling properties and doubling your portfolio every five years.

A stellar management team handles the day-to-day business of property ownership and rentals. You maintain the control, check in monthly on your investments, and make executive decisions on buying and selling. Then, you let your trusted team do the rest, thereby reducing your time commitment to a few hours a month.

7. Combined Interest That Creates Double-Digit ROIs
Making Financial Freedom a Reality

I saved the best for last because this one is my absolute favorite!

Every year you collect cash flow, your property appreciates, and your renters pay down the mortgage. All of this can combine together to form an impressive ROI that outpaces all traditional investments. This section is a little longer because we'll need to calculate the *net positive monthly cash flow*. You will need this number (it's the amount that goes into your pocket after rent is collected and all expenses are paid) to calculate each of the three ROIs we will then be combining later in the example. Here is a quick reminder of the ROI formula to use for our calculations:

TOTAL ROI

$$\frac{\text{TOTAL GAIN}}{\text{TOTAL INVESTMENT}} \times 100 = \text{TOTAL ROI}$$

First up is the net cash flow calculation:

COMBINED INTEREST IN ACTION:

You purchase a single-family home for $200,000. You make a 20 percent down payment of $40,000, plus pay $10,000 in closing costs and reserves for a total investment of $50,000. Let's evaluate how three financial benefits combine to form a 25 percent ROI on this property. Here are the relevant numbers:

Purchase price: $200,000

Down payment (20 percent): $40,000

Closing costs and reserves: $10,000

Total investment ($40,000 + $10,000): $50,000

Monthly rent (what tenant pays): $1,600

Monthly mortgage payment: $1,000

Gross positive monthly cash flow
($1,600 mortgage – $1,000 rent): $600

Net positive monthly cash flow:
$600 monthly cash flow – $267 expenses = $333
(expenses include monthly breakdown of property tax, property insurance, property management fees, repairs, and vacancies).

So, now let's calculate our ROIs based on these figures.

1. Cash-on-Cash ROI: 8 percent
This ROI takes into account the positive cash flow you earn after using rent to pay expenses on the property.

To calculate ROI, we'll need the total gain for the year (or the yearly positive cash flow):

> **Total gain: $333 net positive cash flow**
> **x 12 months = $4,000**

So, now we can calculate ROI:

> **$4,000 total gain / $50,000 total investment**
> **x 100 = 8 percent cash-on-cash ROI**

2. Principal Reduction ROI: 5 percent
This ROI comes from your renters paying the mortgage every month.

With a 30-year mortgage, a portion of each payment to the bank goes towards *interest*. A portion also goes towards paying down the *principal*. I love having tenants help pay down my principal because someday I will sell the house and receive tremendous gain because of it. This factors into a part of my total ROI.

The math is a little complex on this one because of the way banks do their *amortization schedules*. (An amortization schedule shows how much money you pay in principal and interest over time.)

But on average, for a 30-year mortgage of a house priced below the median, the *annual principal reduction ROI is 5 percent.*

3. Appreciation ROI: 12 percent
This ROI comes from the value of the home increasing over time.

For more than 50 years, the average home value in America has increased 4.85 percent annually. Let's assume for the sake of being conservative that the home in this example is appreciating at 3 percent.

To calculate appreciation ROI, we need to determine the annual appreciation:

> *Annual appreciation: $200,000 property value*
> *x 3 percent (.03) = $6,000 annual appreciation*

So, how does this figure into my Appreciation ROI?

If the home increases $6,000 in value over a year, let's use our trusted ROI formula once again to do the math:

> *$6,000 total annual appreciation*
> */ $50,000 total investment x 100*
> *= 12 percent appreciation ROI*

4. Total Combined ROI: 8 + 5 + 12 = 25 percent
This ROI comes from adding together the separate ROIs on the investment.

The math is simple on this one. We're just adding together the three previous ROIs we calculated:

> *8 percent cash-on-cash ROI*
> *+ 5 percent principal reduction ROI*
> *+ 12 percent appreciation ROI*
> *= 25 PERCENT TOTAL ROI*

I truly hope this straightforward example and simple math accurately demonstrates how real estate provides stable and predictable double-digit ROIs when you combine all the ways you make money on your portfolio.

② Potential Energy Ingredient #2
The Six Criteria for Selecting the Best Strategy

Understanding *why* real estate is beneficial is one matter. Learning what strategies will make each of these benefits work for you is a different matter altogether. When I started my real estate journey, my mentors were engaged in a cornucopia of real estate transactions, from flips and foreclosures to land development and commercial deals.

I quickly became obsessed with determining which of these real estate strategies was best. I needed some answers!

So, first, I asked my mentors which strategies they recommended. Imagine my disappointment when none of them would give me a definitive response. They all said it depended on what I "valued most."

Ugh! What does that even mean? Well, turns out it's actually pretty straightforward:

I had to decide my priorities that fit the unique goals that I set and the expectations I had for investing in real estate.

The most profitable strategy might also be the riskiest, or be more time-intensive than you bargained for. You may be more or less risk averse than the next guy. You might want to be a hands-on real estate investor and save money by doing all of the day-to-day management, or you might want to buy real estate from a beach in Tahiti.

After I realized how these different expectations changed the type of real estate investor I would be, I did some soul searching and asked myself what my investing standards were (or, in other words, what priorities were driving the sports car). I came up with six criteria, and then I measured where I fell on each spectrum:

1. Time Investment: LOW

Do you want a strategy that uses a majority of the workweek or the bare minimum?

I was looking for investments that required the absolute *least* amount of my time. I was not interested in being a landlord. I would gladly pay someone else to do the day-to-day work of managing my properties.

2. Effort Investment: LOW

Do you want management of the property to be complex or easy?

I am always interested in the least amount of effort. I don't want a property that is so high maintenance it causes my total ROIs to decrease from the sheer amount of effort it takes to manage it.

3. Risk Level: LOW

Do you want the most risk or the least risk?

I find comfort in knowing that there is the least risk possible in most market conditions.

4. Profit Level: HIGH

Do you want it to make a lot of money or just enough to supplement your income?

I was seeking a way to make enough to quit my job. So, yes, I wanted the most profit possible.

5. Market Conditions: ANY

Do you want your investments to work in only good markets or in all markets?

The properties I selected must provide double-digit ROI in both up and down markets since my plan was to leave my job and rely on cash flows from real estate to fund my lifestyle.

6. Provide Value: ALWAYS

Do I want it to help or hurt people?

I know this one seems like a no-brainer. Still, anyone who has ever dealt with unethical or dishonest people knows that providing value to others is not at the top of everyone's list. For me, any transaction in which I engage must offer a valuable service or benefit to myself and others.

After I determined where I landed on each spectrum, I compared the top thirty real estate strategies against each other based on these criteria. I then selected the real estate strategy that I've now been using with massive success for eighteen years in all market conditions.

Ready for it? Good, because it's ingredient number three.

 Potential Energy Ingredient #3

The Number One Strategy for Building Your Portfolio

Based on these six criteria, a reliable strategy with massive returns emerged, and it's now the one I teach all of my coaching clients.

> **MY WINNING REAL ESTATE STRATEGY:**
> Purchase entry-level single-family homes, in the best markets, below the median, with a short-term buy and hold of approximately five years.

This is *the* strategy I used to create financial freedom by my mid-twenties and has since allowed me to grow a nationwide team of 200 experts who help other investors utilize this same strategy. Let's take a closer look at each of the *four elements* of my strategy that work together to make it so effective at consistently producing double-digit ROIs.

Element 1: Purchase entry-level single-family homes.

Entry-level, single-family homes represent the American dream—the most popular real estate, always in the highest demand. We're talking about three-to-four bedroom, one-to-two-bathroom homes in desirable neighborhoods (nice schools, low crime rate, American suburbia).

Element 2: Purchase below the median.

If you purchase homes below the median, you will possess the most desirable real estate with the greatest demand. This price range also experiences the most significant growth.

The simplest way to think about median home price is what the average person can afford. From the time the housing market recovered after the 2008 bubble burst until about mid-2020, the median home price hovered near $250,000. Since then, it has risen and is expected to continue doing so. But, even when another correction happens, remember that this investing strategy is designed to work in *all* market conditions.

Being under the median also keeps you reasonably safe from a recession. Homes above the median decrease the most in value (as we saw earlier, with the massive losses the most expensive homes take in a down economy). In a downturn, single-family homes below the median are the most resilient. In a sense, they are "recession proof" given that in a down economy, middle America will still need places to live.

Element 3: Purchase in the best markets.

Most investors purchase homes in their backyard, and indeed, you can find great deals nearby. However, suppose you have saved a considerable amount in your armored truck and want to consistently access only the *highest* ROIs. In that case, you will need to invest in the markets nationwide that have the best advantages (and you may or may not be living in one of those markets).

After buying and selling my first round of properties, I determined that the amount of time it took to manage the homes in my backyard required more time than I was willing to invest. I wanted passive—not active—real estate investments.

So, I did some experimenting and discovered something interesting: Owning rentals in the top-performing, out-of-state markets earned the *same* double-digit ROIs as my local lease options. However, the national strategy ended up being the more passive of the two.

And we have a winner! I'll take the more passive investing option every time.

The U.S. has over 324 defined real estate markets. A select number of these markets at any given time are experiencing the highest population increase, migration, and job growth (all great things for rental property owners). Markets also vary in other macro-economic forces that determine how well your investments produce cash flow and appreciate.

Every five to ten years, the top markets shift to different parts of the country. It's essential to keep up with the changes and know where your investment dollars will have the most impact. To learn more about the current top three markets, go to **KrisKrohn.com/Markets**.

Element 4: Utilize a short-term buy and hold.

The highest profitability on a single-family home occurs in the first five years of the hold before your ROI begins to diminish. As a result, I generally sell off and multiply my portfolio every four to seven years.

The ultimate goal is to double my portfolio every five years on average. If I start with five homes today, my goal is to trade them for ten houses within the next five years, give or take a year.

> ### WHAT IS BUY AND HOLD REAL ESTATE?
> "Buy and hold real estate" is an investment strategy where an investor *buys* a property and *holds* it for an extended period of time (rather than, say, buying the property and flipping it right away). When you utilize my strategy, you will be selling a property within four to seven years of purchasing it. But in the meantime, it will be a source of cash flow, tax benefits, and appreciation.

Understanding the seven benefits of real estate investing and the six criteria for selecting the best strategy led to my customized strategy that works for most real estate investors.

When I was brand new to the real estate game, I set my goal at 20 homes with approximately $500 each of cash flow to produce $10,000 a month. That was the magic number that allowed me to quit my job and be well on my way toward creating financial freedom.

And the rest, as they say, is history.

It only takes that first property to get you hooked. Once you experience it, the feeling of making money while you sleep is one that you will not want to live without.

Which Path Should You Take?

The more investors I worked with over the years, the more I discovered there are ultimately two things that determine what kind of investor you will be:

1. The amount of capital you have.

2. The level of involvement you want (active vs. passive).

GOT MONEY TO INVEST

With this graphic, you can see how straightforward it is to determine the path you should take based on those two factors (whether you have money to invest and how involved you wish to be). By using the diagram—along with the criteria in this chapter—you will be able to more easily decide if you will look for properties locally or expand your search nationwide. You will also have a good idea as to whether lease options or rentals suit you best.

Here is a little more about the four possible investing paths:

Path #1

No Money + Hands On (Active)

If you wish to be hands-on in real estate but have no savings to invest, focus on local lease option deals. Whether you have the money to buy real estate really doesn't matter—there's always a way to buy if you have the proper training and the right mentor. I started with almost nothing and built a meaningful portfolio with this local lease option strategy. I explain this in detail in my book, *The Strait Path to Real Estate Wealth*.

Path #2

No Money + Hands Off (Passive)

If you have no savings to invest and no interest in being actively involved with your properties, I have good news. In Chapter Nine, I will reveal how to leverage strategic partnerships to purchase property with other people's capital. You will also discover how you can partner with me and leverage my track record.

Path #3

Money + Hands On (Active)

Once again, the lease option strategy is the way to go. It allows you to mix little to no-money-down, seller-financing deals that don't require a bank with standard investment deals that require as much as 20 to 25 percent down. If you want to learn about executing a local lease-option strategy in one hour, check out my digital master class, "How to Make $5K In 30 Days," which breaks everything down for you. You can sign up at: **KrisKrohn.com/LeaseOption**. No matter how much savings you have, this class will help you jump into the active real estate game.

Path #4

Money + Hands Off (Passive)

When you have money to invest but don't want to be involved, your ideal strategy will include buying properties in the top five markets in the country. Successful investors know that the people they choose to surround themselves with make the difference between fleeting luck and sustainable success. That is why I began developing a team that I couldn't find anywhere else. As I continued leveraging a passive strategy to build my wealth, I discovered that my team could facilitate more deals in the hottest nationwide markets than I could ever possibly purchase independently. That's when we created the concept of becoming facilitators for other real estate investors, from newbies to the most experienced.

Today, my team of over 200 experts facilitate the best deals for me in the top five markets. People also partner with me from all over the world as passive investors. They put up the capital, my team does all the work, and we split everything. To learn more from my investment team about building a winning portfolio, contact us at **KrisKrohn.com/Portfolio**.

Whether you do or don't have money to invest in real estate and no matter what level of involvement sounds most appealing, there is a real estate path made just for you! To learn more about how to enact a hands-on versus a hands-off strategy, check out the Bonus entitled, "What's Your Real Estate Style?" at **KrisKrohn.com/Style**.

Excuses are Rooted in Fear

It's easy to assume that lack of knowledge, money, luck, or timing are the reasons why people give up on real estate investing. Surprisingly, that's not the case. Those are just excuses people tell themselves to justify their decisions to jump ship. Don't sell yourself short! The reality is most people *do* have what it takes. So, before we conclude this powerful chapter, we need to address the elephant in the room.

I'm talking, of course, about a little thing known as *fear*. The only time fear serves any purpose is when you're in danger (being chased by a mountain lion would qualify). Other than that, fear is harmful.

Fear stifles dreams, dampens bright futures, and robs you of joy.

Still, I know what you're thinking: *What if?*

1. What if I lose all my money?

2. What if the economy tanks?

3. What if one of my properties stays vacant too long?

4. What if my tenant hammers my property?

5. What if I fail?

All of those "what ifs" represent so much fear! From my research and from thousands of conversations over the years, I have discovered the top five reasons why real estate fails to deliver for many who dabble in it. *Spoiler alert:* These reasons are all based on emotions like fear, not logic!

1. They give up way too soon.

From a young age, we are programmed to quit when things get tough. Somewhere in our pre-teen or teenage years, people start telling us we can't do big things, and, for some reason, we actually *believe* them. So, we try something a few times, and if it fails to deliver, we chalk it up as an inevitable failure.

You fail, assume you're "just no good" at this investing thing, and give up. Let me tell you that you are capable of doing so much more. Real success in life takes more than a few attempts!

The number one reason for real estate failure is giving up too soon. Don't be a quitter! Trust the process.

2. They lack motivation.

You need practice and training to stretch outside of your comfort zone, to go above and beyond. You also need a reason to make that effort. You have to be able to see what that effort will bring. You have to recognize that the steps you take now will bring you financial freedom in the not-too-distant future. You have to want that freedom.

3. They doubt their abilities.

Self-doubt can be one of our biggest enemies, and if you're hanging around with the wrong people—people who don't push you to go further—then you need to find some new friends. You CAN do this.

4. They assume the worst.

If you believe you're going to fail, then I promise you this: You will be correct. What we think, we become. So, tell yourself that you can keep going no matter what! You *will* get there.

5. They exhibit wrong thinking.

Everything goes back to mindset. *Everything.*

The most important real estate you own is between your ears. Train your mind. Tell yourself that you can do anything and everything. A coach or mentor can see what you can't see, so find one and trust them. Lone wolves die—alone. With the right mindset and help from a capable mentor, you can be more than you realize.

When you move past your fears, you'll realize just how much there is to gain by investing in real estate. But (and this is a big but) it has to be done right. In my book, *The Strait Path to Real Estate Wealth,* I document the journey that enabled me to arrive at the battle-tested real estate strategy we just discussed.

It's critical to select the proper real estate strategy and set it in motion. It's the only proven way to immediately start earning double-digit returns on the money you have in your reserve vehicle.

Even if you aren't sure what kind of investor you want to be (active or passive, local or national), start building your real estate portfolio now. Don't wait!

If you think double-digit ROIs are impressive, you're going to love the next chapter. I'll show you how to shift to a triple-digit ROI by doing the opposite of what most investors do—by leveraging more risk, not less!

Let's keep going, and we're only going to pick up the pace from here.

CHAPTER SIX CHECKPOINT

1. Within a year of investing in real estate, I was hooked, thanks to massive double-digit ROI and increased cash flow.

2. Real estate investing is only as lucrative as you make it with the: 1) reserves you bring to the table, and 2) the knowledge you gain, ideally from an expert mentor in the industry.

3. Real estate investing has seven benefits: appreciation, cash flow, leverage control, tax benefits, market resilience, passive investing, and combined ROIs.

4. There are six criteria to consider when selecting the right real estate strategy for you: time investment, effort investment, risk comfort level, profit goals, market conditions, and desired value.

5. After years of research and experimentation, I determined the ideal strategy for building a passive real estate portfolio is to purchase single-family homes below the median in the nation's best markets on a short-term buy and hold.

6. The type of investor you will be is determined by your available capital and the level of involvement you wish to have (active vs. passive investing).

Given a 10 percent chance
of a 100 times payoff,
you should take
that bet every time.

SEVEN

YOUR ASYMMETRIC RISK VEHICLE

Triple-Digit ROI

I REMEMBER WELL THE THRILL of Friday nights as a kid, primarily because of two words:

Blockbuster Video.

If you were blessed to be a child of the 1980s as I was, there is no doubt you can recall the feeling of going to Blockbuster. You pulled up and gazed across the parking lot at that glorious blue and yellow sign, a beacon of entertainment beckoning you to come try out a new cinematic delight.

As you walked inside, fluorescent lights illuminated the towering wall of new releases (and the center aisles filled with old favorites). There was always that worn-out copy of *Caddyshack*. Then there was *E.T.*, *Back to the Future*, and anything by John Hughes. When in doubt, you could always fall back on the *Star Wars* trilogy (there used to only be three *Star Wars* movies, not 287 like there are now).

I remember the first time I saw DVDs sitting beside the VHS copies of some of the classics. I stood in amazement, wondering how in the world such a thin, tiny disc held an entire film.

Back in those days, there was no button on your remote that brought movies up in two seconds. There were no smartphones with 100 different movie apps (the only mobile phones we had required actual *bags* to carry the giant phones and chargers). No, you went to Blockbuster, browsed, and bought Twizzlers and root beer while you were at it.

Imagine my surprise when I first heard about this new company that mailed movies to you, and then you sent them right back! *What sorcery is this?* Who could have ever imagined such a fanciful concept?

Apparently, Netflix did. Because even before their streaming service, Netflix had sealed Blockbuster's fate simply by figuring out a way to rent movies via snail mail. Netflix became the standard for what it means to be an *industry disruptor*. And for those savvy investors who bought a slice of the Netflix pie early in the game, their ROIs were in the five digits by the mid-2015 stock split.

Imagine that you could go back to 2014 and purchase stock in Netflix before their ROI increased by 23,865 percent. That means:

If you had bought $1,000 worth of shares in Netflix in 2014, you'd have made over $230,000.

What if you had predicted that Amazon would become the e-commerce hub for the planet, and it would grow more than 21,487 percent? What if you had anticipated that Shopify was going to help small-shop owners worldwide sell their products. And because of that, it would grow 6,717 percent?

With the benefit of hindsight, it's easy for us to say, "Well, of course those are winners!" But when these companies were first emerging, investing in them would have seemed like a *risky* bet to most people.

Risk—it's a word that elicits many different reactions depending on how much you know about it and how you are wired. So, let's talk about the word *risk* and why the planet's wealthiest people *actively* seek it out.

Risk: The World's Greatest Investing Tool

Our bodies are innately designed to respond to risky situations in two ways: fight or flight. So, in a nutshell, risk either makes people run screaming in the other direction, or it makes them plant their feet in the arena like Russell Crowe in *Gladiator*.

Me? I'm an arena guy.

That's why I became obsessed with the concept in this chapter when one of my mentors, the legendary Ray Dalio, first explained it to me. Risk is the stuff that makes life worthwhile. Some people jump out of airplanes. I buy shares in exciting companies within emerging markets.

I highly value risk, as long as it meets two requirements: It has to be *intelligent*, and it has to have a *huge potential payoff.* We're talking about **race-car-speed growth**—three-digit and higher returns. That makes it the third vehicle on our Financial Freedom Roadmap. Here is our roadmap again for a reminder of where we are on the path to financial freedom.

FINANCIAL FREEDOM ROADMAP

① RESERVE

Save 20% of your income in your single-digit ROI account.

Financial Reserve Vehicle

Single-digit ROI

② INVEST

Invest reserves into high ROI vehicles.

③ CONVERT

Create lifestyle cash flow through high ROIs and reinvest.

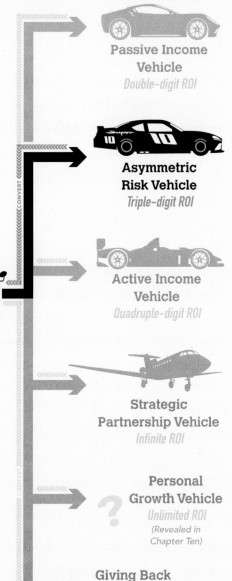

Passive Income Vehicle

Double-digit ROI

Asymmetric Risk Vehicle

Triple-digit ROI

Active Income Vehicle

Quadruple-digit ROI

Strategic Partnership Vehicle

Infinite ROI

Personal Growth Vehicle

Unlimited ROI
(Revealed in Chapter Ten)

Giving Back

Incalcuable ROI
(Revealed in Chapter Eleven)

The most intelligent risks are also going to be *high-risk*. The reason is that low-risk investments guarantee failure. I don't invest in failure. I invest in winning, which is why I actively seek out the highest risk investments.

> ## HOW DO TRADITIONAL INVESTMENTS FAIL?
>
> Low-risk investments guarantee failure, but it's not "failure" in the traditional sense. If you have a certain goal for retirement or financial freedom, and that goal requires double-digit returns or greater to get you there, what do you call it if your returns are too low to compound and get you to your desired end result? I call that failure.
>
> If your plan is guaranteed to not hit the goal, then it's a broken plan. If your average ROIs are too low across the board, you'll never make it to your goal, and you're actually guaranteed to fail. If the plan or aggregate ROI is broken out the gate ... don't do it.

The kiddie pool is shallow. You can swim in it (sort of), and the upside is it's tough to drown (but not impossible). It's also boring. I want to be able to dive in and swim freely. There is an inherent danger to swimming in deeper waters. But that danger is necessary if you desire the financial freedom it takes to have it all. So, yes ...

This chapter is about taking the kind of risks where you could lose.

Honestly, though? This isn't as scary as it sounds. I can't *guarantee* anything, and neither can anyone else. It's not even a guarantee that you'll wake up in the morning. However, the numbers (i.e., the high returns you want) heavily favor intelligent risk.

Buying stock in someone else's business is all about *leverage*. You invest a little, other people do all the work to turn a profit, and you get to reap a percentage of the rewards.

It *almost* sounds too good to be true if we didn't already know this is how the stock market actually works.

Now, I hesitate to even use the term "stock market."

The phrase means something entirely different to me than it does to everyone else. Most people equate stock market investing with the S&P 500, IRAs, index funds, mutual funds—everything I absolutely *can't stand*. People think they are ultra-diversified and cleverly hedging their risk by using "so many different types of investments."

Let's think about that logic for a second. Every one of those vehicles I just listed banks its success on the exact same thing—owning a bunch of minuscule fragments of the world's biggest companies.

How diversified does that sound?

When you think about it, that is literally the *opposite* of "diversified." It's also a sign that someone really doesn't understand the concept of using risk as an investment tool.

Ray Dalio is the founder of the world's largest hedge fund firm, Bridgewater Associates. He has successfully managed over $140 billion for his stock market investors over the years. One of the best things he ever told me is this:

"Having 15 different asset classes eliminates 85 percent of your risk."

In this book, we're only talking about four different asset classes. Yes, there are many more—and the more ways you seek to diversify, the better. So, it's time to face the music by hearing this truth: Having multiple investments based on blue-chip stocks is not "being diversified." It's also ironically pretty risky (and not the intelligent kind).

Owning multiple versions of indexes is what I consider *no diversification* at all. Even when you "win big," let's be honest—it's a pretty small win (especially now that you are learning how many other great investment vehicles exist). However, owning multiple slices of various up-and-coming companies in an assortment of emerging industries *is diversification* in multiple asset classes.

I would rather have a slice of watermelon than an entire grape!

For me, here is what investing in the stock market is:

> **STOCK MARKET (INVESTMENT VEHICLE):**
> Carefully picking companies that you believe in and want to own. It's about investing in winners who will redefine the future—not for 10 percent or even 100 percent returns. Owning a piece of a company should create mid-three-digit and higher ROIs.

I love the stock market because I *live* for the thrill of buying, building, and selling businesses. That is, in essence, what you're doing when you buy and sell shares. And I'm gonna let you in on a little secret: The world's wealthiest people are *business owners*. They own their own businesses and a stake in the businesses of many others.

I'm a passionate "business ownership enthusiast." If you aren't yet, I'd consider becoming one.

I have attempted multiple times to build thriving, successful businesses, and it's never been easy. I've had my share of successes, but can those wins compare to those of up-and-coming industry leaders that will eventually be household names? No, don't delude yourself —the winning approach is to own *multiple* businesses, including your own.

Of course, if it were as easy as "own a piece of other companies and get rich," then there'd be no need for this chapter. So, if it isn't already clear, allow me to clarify: We are not talking about the standard methods of investing such as mutual funds, index funds, 401(k)s, IRAs, or the S&P 500. You'll never earn multi-digit ROIs with the obvious winners (more on that in Step 1 of The Asymmetric Risk Investing System on page 151).

The Boring Way vs. the Better Way

The S&P 500 consists of the *most successful* 500 publicly traded companies on the planet with the absolute *highest* ROIs in profits. And yet, investing in these giants doesn't earn the average investor anything above single digits over an investment's lifetime! But people do it every day because it's safe and predictable.

Seriously, why even bother?

The most accelerated path to wealth is not littered with teeny tiny fragments of huge companies. These only serve to bring your risk so low that your ROI drops to single digits. This conventional type of investment strategy utilizes *symmetric risk* exposure.

SYMMETRIC RISK (NOUN):
The low risk associated with traditional investing that delivers lackluster returns but promises safety in the sense that potential gain and loss *equal* each other (hence, symmetric).

Here is a classic example of symmetric risk:

You bet $100 on a coin toss. If it lands on heads, you win $100, but if it lands on tails, you lose $100. Because the potential gain and loss equal each other, you are facing a symmetric risk exposure.

People are always talking about work-life *balance* and a *balanced* portfolio. We shun asymmetry and seek equilibrium. Look at these two images and tell me which one your brain likes better. The one on the right looks lumpy and less appealing. Maybe you feel the urge to fix it or re-draw it.

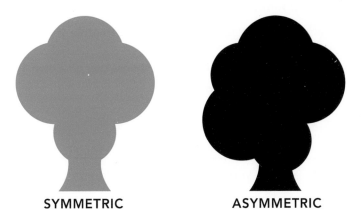

SYMMETRIC   **ASYMMETRIC**

And yet, most great art is asymmetrical, often profoundly so. Artists call this *asymmetrical balance*. Think about the works of Van Gogh and Picasso—not an ounce of traditional symmetry to be found.

So, maybe asymmetry isn't so bad after all. In fact, we should strive for asymmetry when it comes to the stock market.

ASYMMETRIC RISK (NOUN):
The intelligent risk an investor faces when targeting investments with high upsides and low downsides.

Remember the Netflix example from earlier in the chapter, where a $1,000 investment in 2014 increased to $230,000? Well, if Netflix went to zero, you would be out $1,000, but instead it went up 230 times. This is a classic example of low downside (losing your small investment) and high upside (multiplying your money many times over).

In the 1949 book, *The Intelligent Investor*, Benjamin Graham, the father of value investing, said, "The essence of portfolio management is the management of risks, not returns."

Traditional investors focus on returns rather than risk. By focusing both on the risks *and* returns, you can find ways to maximize your returns while you simultaneously minimize your risks. In other words:

When you utilize asymmetric risk, your shares can go down 100 percent, but their growth is unlimited.

Asymmetric risk is an *intelligent* risk because it looks at the big picture and systematically weighs the pros and cons. Using an established system enables you to rely not on emotion or hunches but on research, logic, and mathematics.

That said, there is still a place for "safe" traditional investments that provide a stable return. It's for those who are already extremely wealthy. When people with large sums of money do not require growth but consistency, they can turn to single-digit ROI models. However, it is not for those who are in the wealth-accumulation phase.

The Quest for Moonshots

Ironically, asymmetric risk also relies on *losing* as a fundamental part of the strategy. If you do it correctly, you will lose a majority of the time, which also means that it has to be money you are willing to lose.

It's counterintuitive, to be sure.

So, how did Ray Dalio become one of the most successful hedge fund managers of all time through the use of asymmetric risk? He explained the principle to me in a simple manner:

Imagine you have $500 to invest in the stock market. After some research, you discover five companies who meet all of your criteria for asymmetric risk investments but are not yet in the spotlight. Let's assume your criteria of asymmetric risk is to pick companies that can go up 500 percent or multiply five times. You invest $100 in each of the five companies. Here is the end result:

1. $100 investment #1: $0 return

2. $100 investment #2: $0 return

3. $100 investment #3: $0 return

4. $100 investment #4: $0 return

5. $100 investment #5: $500 return

With that one investment split five ways, you created a 500 percent ROI on one of your $100 investments. You also broke even. And you accomplished this even though four out of the five investments were total duds.

Now imagine that *two* of your $100 investments each delivered a 500 percent ROI. In other words, both produced $500.

So, you took the initial $500 (the total investment spread out over five companies) and made a total of $1,000 despite losing $300 out of your original $500 investment.

This represents a net 100 percent ROI.

In essence, you have doubled your money despite *losing* out on three out of five of your investments! Let me say that again: **You doubled your money even though you lost 60 percent of your bets.** That is the essence of asymmetric risk exposure, and it's brilliant.

The key in this example is that the two investments that won were 500 percent ROI investments. In reality, the higher the potential ROI, the better (and 500 percent is just the beginning).

The higher the upside, the less the downside risk.

This isn't day trading. This is a logical commitment to adhering to a strict philosophy that requires research and patience. In other words, this is allocating a percentage of your reserve vehicle to invest in *moonshots*.

> ### MOONSHOT (NOUN):
> An ambitious, exploratory project that possesses little expectation of short-term profitability. In the long-term, however (five to 10 years), there is a clear expectation of at least a 10,000 percent ROI because the company increases 100 times in value.

If you know how to harness moonshots, then asymmetric risk can generate triple-digit and higher ROIs. However, I need to make an important distinction. This is not a "pick one horse and bet the farm" strategy. That's foolish—and that's what gamblers do.

The majority of your picks won't be 10,000 percent-ROI moonshots, and that's okay. The key is to take your total investment and spread it out (more on that in just a minute).

If you think it's impossible to find companies with such potential, I'd like to ask you to think bigger. You also need to break out from that tiny box your conventional financial planner stuck you into years ago. He put you in there with the vehicles that make *him* the most money and leave *you* disappointed. Once you step outside that box, you will realize that there is a more intelligent and faster way.

The Asymmetric Risk Investing System

Investing in companies in emerging industries is what the world's richest men and women do every day. It's not a theory, and it's not an idea. It's standard practice for the wealthy. Make no mistake:

These are the steps the wealthy take. These are the rules the rich live by and how they craft their legacies.

To put this asymmetric risk into action, here's what Ray Dalio would tell you to do. It's a system that involves five steps.

① Do your research.

I'm amazed by interviews with former CIA operatives and spies when they talk about being able to walk into *any* situation and know, within just moments, where exits are, how many people are in the room and approximate ages and heights, who looks suspicious, and more.

Being an adherent to an asymmetric risk philosophy requires you to become an enthusiastic, intelligent, and keen observer. Moonshots don't just appear. You have to know where to look for them. You need to see not where things are now but where things are going.

I'm talking about finding future-focused startups and emerging industries in their relative infancy *today* that will dominate the world *tomorrow*. The question then becomes:

Who will be the most influential disruptors within the next decade?

Disruption is a buzzword—and for good reason. It's the key to find-ing high-ROI investments! Think about the disruption Uber created in the world of transportation. Taxis have been on the streets since the 1880s. And yet, since 2017, without owning a single vehicle, Uber gives more rides a day than all the taxi services combined.

Without owning a single piece of real estate, Airbnb rules the hospi-tality industry.

Without owning a single physical movie, Netflix rules the film industry.

Look to the industries that are changing life itself and the way we live it. For example, here some things to consider:

- Tesla has paved the way for electric vehicles to become the standard. But, who else is in the running to become a household name? Think about this: Who will win the contract once the gov-ernment decides to make all government-issued vehicles electric?

- What happens when we replace semi-trucks with electric semis that drive themselves, and who will be responsible for making this happen?

- Who are the up-and-coming players in cryptocurrency, and what will they do to the way we buy and sell *everything*?

- Who is responsible for bringing 5G to the world, and what compa-nies are developing 6G? It's coming sooner than you think. Within a few years, you'll be able to download an entire movie in five sec-onds. You need to find out who is going to be responsible for that.

- Artificial intelligence (AI) is changing the world, from manu-facturing to the tech industry and beyond. Who are the most exciting AI players, and what are they doing today to generate five-digit ROIs within a decade?

- The medical field is being transformed through rapidly emerging areas like augmented reality (AR) for operating rooms, telehealth, biotech, and genetic engineering. Which companies are starting to stand out as disruptors in these spaces?

The most intelligent stock market investments aren't going to be in your face. They aren't the ones offered at your neighborhood investment firm, and they're not making headlines all day long. Companies with prominent visionaries at the helm are already in the spotlight—and the thing about the spotlight is that everybody else can see it, too.

Avoid companies with well-established high book value, stable cash flow, and high current share price. In contrast, the most significant indicator of high and promising upside potential is anticipated or projected earnings.

I'm not asking you to become a fortune teller, and you don't need magical skills to see into the future. There are plenty of tangible signs of future success for those who know what to look for. Look to the future—and you do this by leveraging emerging market research firms that know:

- *Who* tomorrow's star players will be.

- *What* kinds of earnings you can reasonably expect.

- *When* you can expect moonshots to start producing these returns.

- *Where* these players will emerge.

- *Why* the risk is more than worth the reward.

That is how it's done.

ACTION STEP! ▶ I recommend you align with research services that study future niches and share their findings. Every year, I spend thousands on research services and then I turn their advice into significant returns.

You can research yourself or leverage the knowledge, insight, and analysis of others—*leverage rocks!*

② Pick wisely.

After aligning yourself with research firms who are constantly searching for moonshots, pick 15 of the most explosive, under-the-radar companies showing a 10,000 percent potential ROI. This means if the projections are correct, those investments will grow 100 times in value during your ownership.

Because you can invest in thousands of companies (thanks to the ease and accessibility of online trading), there are plenty of opportunities to discover investments that have the combination you want:

Limited downside with tremendous upside potential.

Pick your projected winners and spread out your allotted investment evenly among all 15 of them. If you spread your investment equally amongst 15 opportunities, each with 10,000 percent ROI potential, and 12 of your 15 picks fail but three succeed, here is how you win:

DETAILS:
15 investments ($1,000 each) = $15,000 total investment
Time period: 5 years

RESULT:
12 investments fail, 3 investments win.

The three winners each have a 10,000% (100x) ROI:

$1,000 Investment #1 = $100,000 (100x growth)
$1,000 Investment #2 = $100,000 (100x growth)
$1,000 Investment #3 = $100,000 (100x growth)

Total earned after 5 years = $300,000
(from a $15,000 investment)

ROIS:

$$\frac{\$300,000 \text{ earnings}}{\$15,000 \text{ investment}} = 20 \times 100 = 2,000\% \text{ TOTAL ROI}$$

$$\frac{2,000\% \text{ Total ROI}}{5 \text{ years}} = 400\% \text{ YEARLY ROI}$$

That's an exciting triple-digit ROI!

Now, it's never this simple. In real life, most failed picks don't go to zero, and not every winner increases 100 times in value. However, you can still reasonably expect mid-three-digit returns by following this strategy.

You need 15 companies that research confirms to have a strong likelihood of being a winner in the future. Remember when investing $1,000 in Netflix would have made you over $230,000?

Why not look for more opportunities like that?

This is not speculation. I have been applying this strategy—and owning a piece of the most exciting and fastest-growing companies—for over a decade.

3 DIY with your selection.

Purchase an equal piece of all 15 companies through a simple online trading platform (many of them are commission-free) rather than a financial planner. Financial planners are greatly incentivized to push only a handful of products. Those are typically the only ones they'll ever share with you. You also have to pay a financial planner, but you skip unnecessary fees if you do it yourself.

So, purchase your share in 15 companies and manage them yourself. This is a passive investment—but doing it yourself is an important reminder that all other experts, tools, and advice are secondary to YOU being in charge and not the other way around. Remember, becoming a self-made millionaire is your responsibility. And while I believe in delegating everything I don't want to do (which is quite a bit), there are some things you simply can't outsource, and this is definitely one of them.

You also need the discipline to divide your money evenly into at least 15 opportunities. No matter how excited you get about a particular company, never favor one over all the others. You are not trying to pick the triple crown winner. This isn't "hunch" work. It's a system that delivers triple-digit ROIs—but only when used correctly.

4 Commit to the plan.

Commit to holding your carefully chosen picks for five to 10 years, focusing on long-term growth before selling.

If you have done your research correctly and allocated your funds equally, this is less risky than it seems. Besides, you are banking on these businesses becoming trailblazers in emerging industries, not fleeting overnight successes. This type of success takes time.

Now, because this is a long-term play, you should only invest money you can afford to lose—because you *will*. But losing is part of winning big.

I admit that this philosophy requires you to mix two different qualities that do not always go together: *boldness* and *patience*. Those two virtues can be like oil and water. I get it. One always seems to be at war with the other. Removing the emotion associated with stock market fluctuations helps a lot in this arena. Hence, the reason for Step 5.

⑤ Rebalance annually.

Every year (not every day, week, or month), rebalance your portfolio and ask whether there's one or two that you should be adding or selling.

We all know people who have the stock app pulled up on their phones constantly, nervously watching every dip and gain, day in and day out. This is not a habit you want or need. You shouldn't be looking at the market every day. Keep the long game in mind.

Don't allow the market to control your feelings. Many years ago, I dabbled in day trading. I was an absolute train wreck when I lost money and was overjoyed when I won. This type of emotion has no place in asymmetric risk investing.

These days, I'm the kind of investor motivated by stock dips! I already know that at least some of my picks will be massive winners (more than enough to offset my losses). So, instead of panic-selling, I buy *more*.

See? I told you this was counterintuitive.

Key Strategy Takeaways

What should you take from this? First, I hope this inspires you to become even more of an excellent saver. Putting the maximum number of dollars into your reserve vehicle should be priority number one.

The reason is that once you do the research, you need to be able to act on opportunities as quickly as possible. You also want to get in on moonshots while they are still affordable.

There is no minimum requirement to get started in either real estate or the stock market.

That's the beauty of both—do it right, and the minimums you need to play the game are low. Find the right real estate deal in the right market, and your initial investments can be minimal. The same is true for the stock market.

Get into the game with minimal investments but still experience high ROIs. It's the best of both worlds, and it's why we focus on the percentages rather than static piles of money as our goals.

A few words of caution as you prepare to gas up your race car and take asymmetric risk for a spin:

1. *Allocate evenly.* If you are putting all of your eggs in one or two baskets, you're doing it wrong. My minimum number of investments is 15 companies.

2. *Invest in research.* This strategy is useless without intelligent analysis. Don't rely on hunches or your cousin Billy's recommendation based on the hot tip he got from Todd in accounting. Find experts and leverage their knowledge and experience.

3. *Quit obsessing.* This strategy does not require any daily consideration. Don't be the obsessive guy at the party who spends his time in the bathroom checking his stocks. Commit to an annual re-balance and know that dips happen (and when the market dips, I double down). *You're playing the long game, not investing in a get-rich-quick scheme.*

4. *Check your emotion.* The moment this becomes emotional, you should get out of the game. You are winning by losing most of the time. If that thought gives you hives, this may not be the right strategy for you.

5. *Never chase the market.* If you are buying only because a stock is on an upward tear, you are reacting to the market. This is a terrifying habit that will lead to major problems over time. Sure, you can experience a few wins this way, but in the long run, it will slaughter your portfolio. Stick to the system.

Here is what you need to remember:

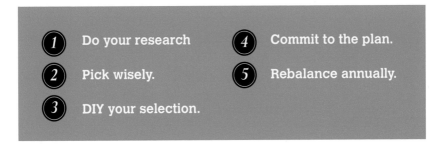

1. Do your research
2. Pick wisely.
3. DIY your selection.
4. Commit to the plan.
5. Rebalance annually.

I regularly interact with my mentors and online investing groups, and I have multiple financial subscriptions that keep me well informed. I also leverage connections to allow me to find the next great opportunity. I am always researching emerging markets and identifying moonshots.

If you'd like free information about my own portfolio, where I go for research, and who helps me stay ahead of the game, or if you want to see more of my passive trading strategies that earn me solid triple digit annual returns, visit: **KrisKrohn.com/Stocks.**

You could put this book down right now and be set for life once you fuel up the first three vehicles in your fleet, but, if you're anything like me, you want to go faster. If that's so, proceed to the next chapter. I will show you an even higher ROI gained when financially successful people leverage business to produce incredible (dare I say "blockbuster" level) returns.

CHAPTER SEVEN CHECKPOINT

1. Risk is inherent in anything with a reward, and the stock market is no exception. That is why, if you want better results than with traditional investments, you have to become a studier of emerging markets and commit to risk.

2. The traditional form of investing is symmetric—the potential gain and loss are *equal* in value. It doesn't utilize the upside of risk and so is lackluster and inefficient.

3. On the other hand, positive asymmetric risk means you're selecting investments with an extraordinarily high upside and low downside period. It's a way to leverage both risk *and* return.

4. The five-step plan for utilizing risk includes leveraging research to identify at least 15 *moonshots* (up-and-comers with potential returns of at least 10,000 percent).

5. After doing your research, DIY purchase stocks in a minimum of 15 companies that you believe will have at least a 10,000 percent ROI.

6. Be prepared to hold these stocks for at least five years before liquidating and commit to a yearly reevaluation rather than obsessing over periodic fluctuations.

If you're trying to
create a company,
it's like baking a cake.
You have to have all
the ingredients in the
right proportion.

ELON MUSK

YOUR ACTIVE
INCOME VEHICLE

Quadruple-Digit ROI

WELCOME TO THE RAT RACE.

Isn't that just about the most depressing sentence you could ever read? Who in their right mind enjoys being likened to a *rat*?

I shudder whenever I hear this comparison. It also makes me sad that people see themselves as faceless cogs in the vicious and never-ending wheel of life. These cogs go through life believing someone else is meant to have control over when and how that wheel moves.

One person who felt trapped in the rat race is my friend Trent. For 10 years, Trent worked tirelessly to build a digital forensic analysis business. Whenever a law enforcement agency or even a concerned spouse felt that someone was embezzling, cheating, or committing a major crime with a traceable digital footprint, they'd call Trent. He would then seize the suspected party's electronics and ultimately prove their guilt or innocence through careful analysis.

He'd seen so much over the years he wished he could forget—things that would live in his mind forever as a reminder of man's depravity. Some of the stories he told me were beyond disturbing. It's mind-blowing to fathom the things that one human being is capable of doing to another. I was disheartened to hear about humanity at its worst, but I was simultaneously captivated by Trent's vigilante-style heroism.

Trent eventually sold his business for various reasons. Then, he decided to stay on to work for the new owner. Trent quickly found himself doing soul-draining work for as many as 80 hours a week. He desperately wanted to escape, but a steady income is a powerful force.

One morning at the gym, Trent looked understandably perplexed as he told me he was about to lose his job and income. The 2020 pandemic had forced cutbacks, and his company could no longer afford his six-figure salary. He had grown to despise the work itself but still relied on the paycheck.

It dawned on Trent that his livelihood was in someone else's hands. He had lost the ability to determine his future path, and it was a helpless feeling. He asked me if I had any ideas. Helping people free themselves from the prison of a thankless job just so happens to be one of my life's greatest passions, so, *obviously*, I had some ideas.

I began to share with Trent some insights about business ownership and how he could be free from his daily grind within a few months. I will share some of that same information here with you, but, just as I asked Trent, I'm going to ask you to promise me three things. These are non-negotiable if you are genuinely interested in becoming the author of your own destiny:

1. Dedicate at least two hours a day to the process.
2. Follow the instructions without wavering.
3. Remain fully committed to the plan.

This chapter will explain the fundamental pieces necessary for a business to bring you an ample *active income*. What do I mean by active? Well, our double-digit and triple-digit ROI vehicles are both fairly *passive incomes*. I made sure to design and present each one in a way that protects your time while still helping you *have it all*, because I truly believe that time is our ultimate asset.

But now, we need to shift gears.

For the first time since we started this journey together, I'm going to ask you to set aside several hours a week. But there's a good reason: This vehicle holds the key to enabling you to leave your current full-time job. Like Trent, 85 percent of our fellow Americans do not like their jobs. So, the odds are you are among those who wish they could find a more fulfilling way to pay the bills and save for retirement.

My financial freedom origin story also began with a desire to exit the rat race. But regardless of whether your goal is to *replace* or *supplement* your income, I want you to understand just how powerful a quadruple-digit ROI can be.

The Rule of 72 helps explain how easy it can be to double your money through an active income vehicle. Here is what I mean (and remember that the Rule of 72 formula is: 72/ROI = time to double your money):

$$72/1{,}000\% \text{ ROI} = .072 \text{ years}$$

$$365 \text{ days} \times .072 = 26 \text{ days}$$

My system for real estate investing can help you become a millionaire within *decades* (thanks to its double-digit returns). Investing in businesses through share ownership and owning your own business are keys to becoming wealthy in *years* (thanks to its triple-digit returns).

But now, thanks to quadruple-digit ROI through active business income, we just went from decades to years to mere *days* required to double your money.

With the proper business standards and processes in place, you can amass wealth through quadruple-digit ROIs without giving up too much of your time. But even more than simply discussing ROI, this chapter will allow you to understand that it *is* possible to tap out of the rat race with the right vehicle (your Formula One race car).

The Real Goal of Business

Whenever we think of people who have crafted their own destiny, the obvious names that come to mind are the rich and famous. Like so many others, I am also inspired by the likes of Oprah Winfrey, Jeff Bezos, J.K. Rowling, and Elon Musk. But you know who *really* inspires me? People like Heather Wright, Nik Krohn (my brother), and

Steven Leavitt. Of course, you don't know who those people are, and *Entertainment Tonight* will never air a special on them. But they are inspiring nonetheless because they did what so few ever do.

They and countless others created financial *and* time freedom through business ownership.

You may be one of the lucky ones and already have a career you love. Sadly, according to a Gallup poll, 85 percent of people absolutely hate what they do for a living. If you feel trapped in a job that brings little fulfillment, then allow me to introduce the fourth vehicle in your financial fleet. This is a vehicle for producing active income through quadruple-digit ROI business investing.

It's your Formula One race car—a vehicle that embodies speed and power.

On the following page is our financial freedom map once again. We're cruising along now at more incredible speeds as we fuel up this fourth vehicle, a powerful machine designed to generate a sizable income to fuel your lifestyle and future investments.

The goal of passive investing (real estate and asymmetric risk investments) is to ensure financial freedom sometime in the future. In contrast, the purpose of active business income (your Formula 1 race car) is to produce a much higher and more immediate ROI that accelerates the financial freedom timeline. But perhaps more importantly, it can unlock the cage that is your full-time schedule and help you reclaim more of your most precious asset.

What exactly am I talking about here?

Well, the word *business* is pretty nebulous, so let's dissect that first. Suppose you ask most people what the goal of any business is. Most

FINANCIAL FREEDOM ROADMAP

 RESERVE

Save 20% of your income in your single-digit ROI account.

Passive Income Vehicle
Double-digit ROI

Asymmetric Risk Vehicle
Triple-digit ROI

Financial Reserve Vehicle
Single-digit ROI

Active Income Vehicle
Quadruple-digit ROI

Strategic Partnership Vehicle
Infinite ROI

 INVEST

Invest reserves into high ROI vehicles.

Personal Growth Vehicle
Unlimited ROI
(Revealed in Chapter Ten)

 CONVERT

Create lifestyle cash flow through high ROIs and reinvest.

Giving Back
Incalcuable ROI
(Revealed in Chapter Eleven)

of their responses will sound something like, "The goal of any business is to produce a profit by solving problems that create value for other people."

While this is certainly not wrong, there is a superior definition, one that factors in the one commodity that is more precious than profits or value creation:

> **THRIVING BUSINESS (NOUN):**
> An endeavor that creates both profit and value without sacrificing too much of the greatest asset—time.

Unfortunately, most business owners end up trading the lion's share of their time for income. This crisis generally arises because entrepreneurs are notorious for wearing two hats at once: owner *and* operator. My goal early on was to be a one-hat entrepreneur. That is, I wanted to become an owner but *not* an operator (sometimes called an "absentee owner"). Yet, this distinction is missing in the accepted definition of *entrepreneurship* today.

One of my business mentors, Keith Cunningham, has launched multiple companies, negotiated numerous million-dollar deals, and structured hundreds of millions of dollars for his business ventures. Possibly my favorite thing that Keith ever said is this:

"Great operators get tired. Great business owners get rich."

You need a business that works for you instead of you working for it. The idea of quitting your day job to "be your own boss" may sound appealing, but if you give up a 40-hour workweek only to work 80 or more hours, is it really worth it?

How much is your time worth to you?

Over the years, I've observed that most people value their time so much that they won't even *consider* starting a business. They hear horror stories of side hustles becoming massive time vacuums, and they are not interested in adding that kind of madness to their lives.

People don't want to miss their Netflix binges and their kids' ball games for a lackluster side gig, and I don't blame them. It can be so emotionally draining and not worth the time trade-off, which is why I need you to understand there is a better way. It requires the following plan of action, which I am going to help you start right here, right now, in this chapter:

> Learn the higher standards of a thriving business. Systematically evaluate every business idea according to the same standards. Work the numbers and don't be afraid of a calculator. Be a stickler for the right profit margin. And don't even think about starting a new venture unless you can automate it.

Becoming Financially Empowered

One of the biggest gambles people make in their wealth plan is banking their entire financial future on a single income source (their 40-hour-workweek job). It's great if your spouse or partner also has a job. But what you really need is to increase the number of *ways* you make money without significantly increasing the amount of time you spend generating that income.

Having *time without money* can be just as suffocating as having *money without time*. True freedom is having both.

If you feel intimidated at the thought of starting a business, let me assure you that you are not alone. Entrepreneurship is scary. It can also be demanding, challenging, and draining (when done improperly). And, in reality, most people fail. This is because they do not have standards for selecting the correct opportunities that lead to maximum ROIs with minimal time commitments.

When it comes to starting a business, people also have many fears that include:

1. Fear of failure.

2. Fear of the unknown.

3. Fear of running out of money.

4. Fear of working too hard or too little.

These fears are not unfounded. According to Investopedia, 20 percent of businesses fail within the first year, 50 percent fail by year five, and 70 percent don't make it to their tenth year in business. To make matters less appealing, the average small business owner makes just $46,000 a year. Another 86 percent of business owners make less than $100,000 a year, and only 2 percent make over $1 million.

There is no denying these are troubling statistics. However, you can avoid most of the mistakes made by new business owners (the ones that lead to the toxic combination of exhaustion and lackluster results) by following the procedures in this chapter before starting a business.

DEVIL'S ADVOCATE

"But Kris, owning a business is way harder than having a job! My entrepre-neur friend works long hours and is way more stressed than I am."

My experience is that even super successful entrepreneurs waste the first decade of their run on bad decisions because they lacked stan-dards. The learning curve of entrepreneurship is steep, and many peo-ple do fail before they figure it out. Learning through trial and error is painful and messy.

MY PROMISE: I will teach you the standards necessary to avoid the years of stress and failure that seem so common in entrepreneurship. When you select a business and operate it according to my business stan-dards, it will shorten your learning curve and reduce the number of mis-takes you make.

If you are one of the many people who believe that working for some-one else is somehow better or more lucrative in the long run, let me ask you a question: *Do you have any idea how much your boss makes on you?* You read that right—because you are, in fact, counted as an asset on your employer's balance sheet. The company invests in you through a wage, and they expect a return.

How much? In general, a company wants to see a 400 percent annual ROI on their investment. The average American makes around $50,000 a year, which means the average employee is expected to help produce $200,000 (or four times their salary).

Well, consider that if a company can own your time and a expect a 400 percent ROI on your skills, then maybe you can, too. Technically, if they earn a 400 percent gain on your skills, then inversely, you should be able to work a quarter (or one-fourth) of the time (translation: work two hours a day) to make the same amount on your own.

I challenge every person I meet who doesn't like their job to seek the answer this riddle,

"How can I make the same amount of money by working two hours a day on my own?"

The answer may not be clear yet, but I'm planting the seed now because this chapter is all about how to replace or supplement your income while reclaiming 75 percent of your time, all in the pursuit of financial freedom measured by money and time.

I have devoted the remainder of this chapter to teaching you some absolutely *critical* knowledge about the world of business ownership so that you can avoid some common and often devastating mistakes. To accomplish this ambitious goal, we will cover three key areas:

1. **How business works.** In this section, we'll discuss the three immutable fundamentals of business success.

2. **How to choose a thriving business.** Once you are acquainted with the success fundamentals, we'll move on to the five standards for selecting a winning business.

3. **How to start a thriving business.** Finally, we'll detail the four essential launch phases of successful business ownership.

Don't make the mistake of starting a side hustle and getting lost in the business, or, even worse, skipping the proper foundations for building a thriving business. Creating an active income stream is supposed to make life better—not make life feel like torture.

By following a distinct set of rules, you can begin to break free from time prison and cultivate a sense of peace and abundance as you become more financially self-reliant.

DEVIL'S ADVOCATE

"Really Kris, you are going to teach me EVERYTHING I need to know about starting a successful business in a single chapter?!"

There's no way I can teach you how to build a successful business in a single chapter, and that isn't my intention. The *real* success of business actually comes down to a handful of standards most people will never be taught, which accounts for their failure. BUT if you learn the things I share in this chapter, you will be equipped with the rules that the most successful business owners use that result in their success.

How Business Works:
The Three Fundamentals

Most people didn't take business classes in college. For those of us who did, we know that those business courses did a lousy job of teaching us how businesses thrive. So, it should come as no surprise to learn that most people don't really understand how business works.

My dad's life as an entrepreneur made business ownership look like the *worst* thing ever. He worked twice as hard as my friends' dads for the same or fewer dollars. There may be entrepreneurs from your childhood or today who paint "being your own boss" in the same negative light. It's not their fault, either. No one teaches us this stuff (crazy but true).

So, let's get back to basics. To develop one or more income streams that have the potential to replace your job, you must understand the three fundamentals of business success:

1. *Marketing*—your ability to generate prospects to buy products or services.

2. *Selling*—your ability to convert those leads into sales.

3. *Fulfillment*—your ability to deliver your product or service.

Businesses must have *marketing* strategies that generate leads (potential customers). Those leads then become paying customers through the *selling* process. After the transaction (exchanging money for a good or service), the business has obligated itself by accepting money to *fulfill* its promise and deliver the product or service.

The cold, hard truth is that as simple as this process sounds, most businesses fail to execute one, two, or all three of these fundamentals correctly. This is why we watch them struggle to survive.

What we'd all prefer to do in life is to *thrive*.

The word *thrive* is full of so much life and energy. Well, the same is true for businesses. There are "thriving" businesses, and there are the typical "surviving" businesses. I consider most businesses to be in survival mode, and that's both sad and unnecessary.

This failure to thrive is most commonly the result of a failure to understand the core principles of business and a lack of knowledge concerning the proper standards that predictably lead to success. We have *widely accepted standards* when it comes to morals. We have *commonly accepted standards* when it comes to relationships.

Yet, we don't have commonly accepted standards when it comes to business. So, we invent our own, but we don't know which standards work or which procedures cause problems. As a result, business owners attempt to reinvent the wheel and learn by constantly failing. How exhausting!

To help illustrate the differences in traditional, failing standards and those used by thriving businesses, we will use two symbols to represent each, as you can see in the exhibit below.

A *surviving* business rubs two sticks together in the freezing cold at the bottom of the mountain. In contrast, a *thriving* business has already climbed to the high summit, conquered the mountain, and celebrates its victory next to a roaring campfire.

SURVIVING VS. THRIVING IN BUSINESS

Surviving Business
Uses no standards, exists in survival mode, and eventually burns out

Survival-mode businesses are notorious time stealers. They also tend to steal joy, destroy relationships, and lead to a life of indentured servanthood to the business.

Thriving Business
Uses proven standards to generate profit, value, and time freedom

Thriving businesses give you back more of your most precious commodity. They also tend to create joy, foster relationships, and lead to a life of financial and time freedom.

Business Fundamental #1: Marketing
The ability to generate leads for your offering.

Almost without exception, you can link a business's success or failure to its ability to generate leads. A *lead* is someone who may or may not be qualified to buy your offering. Gathering leads is the first critical step toward finding *qualified prospects* (those who have the means, ability, and desire to buy what you are selling). Qualified prospects who decide to say yes to your ask become *customers*. The process can be a lot more intricate than that—mainly depending on what you are selling—but that is the basic concept.

You don't open a new business and sit on your hands waiting for customers to walk through the door or stumble onto your website. You have to let people know who you are, where you are, what you do, and how you do it.

Your marketing plan is how this message reaches the world, and it's also how you generate a flowing pipeline of leads.

Here are the glaring differences between the marketing strategies of a surviving business versus a thriving business.

Survival Marketing:

Barely surviving businesses don't know how many leads they have or need to succeed. They approach every day without having the slightest idea where their next customer will come from. Their marketing strategy is less "strategy" and more "luck." A business with too few leads struggles for survival and eventually dies a painful and stressful death.

Thriving Marketing:

A flourishing business has an endless supply of leads, even more than it can sell to. They have figured out a way to create an infinite source of leads and referrals in most market conditions and do so in a sustainable way.

Business Fundamental #2: Selling
The ability to convert leads into sales.

Every revenue-producing transaction in a business requires some type of sale. You don't even have a business until you start selling something. However, selling can be challenging and immensely intimidating depending on the product or service, and because of the stigmas attached to the word itself. Here are the most striking differences between the selling mentality in a surviving business and a thriving business.

Survival Selling:
Business owners mistakenly believe that the mere act of *offering* products or services is the same as *selling*. People only buy from other people and businesses they like, know, and trust—and those factors require intentional effort to manifest. Pushy sales tactics and hard closes are a thing of the past, but some businesses didn't get the memo. You have to work on communicating the value of what you offer to your prospects. Businesses in survival mode also make the mistake of hinging their success on the person's talents doing the selling.

Thriving Selling:
On the other hand, a profitable business has a product in high enough demand that, in many ways, it sells itself (thanks in large part to effective marketing that generates only the best, qualified leads). These are products or services that don't require pushy or high-pressure sales tactics to move. Selling in today's flooded marketplace has to feel natural, comfortable, and rewarding for all parties involved.

Let's talk about a phrase I'm sure you've heard, which is *sales funnel*. The simplest definition of a sales funnel is this:

SALES FUNNEL (NOUN):
The ideal path potential buyers take to become customers. A way to track leads through the four primary sales
stages (from awareness to interest to desire to action)
and align your marketing and sales processes accordingly.
Also called a purchase or conversion funnel.

AWARENESS

INTEREST

DESIRE

ACTION/PURCHASE

Companies spend countless dollars on building an effective funnel that takes all of the leads from their robust lead pipeline generated by their marketing arm, dumps them into the top of the funnel (the wide part), and generates the end result or purchase at the bottom (the narrow spigot).

It sounds so easy, right? Well, it's not quite that simple, partly because there is a lot of misinformation about what works and what doesn't. It doesn't help that everyone and their brother on social media say they have a "proven" system for generating sales, but then you hire them to help you, and they fail to deliver results. *It kinda starts to make you think that no one knows what they're talking about.*

It's also not that simple due to the fact that although *consumer behavior* itself is highly predictable (and is even considered a soft science), that behavior is almost never linear. In other words, not every customer will travel through the four stages in the same order or at the same pace.

Just because it may not be an *exact* science doesn't mean you don't need to develop a funnel system that you never stop testing. You need a well-defined sales funnel in order to:

- Understand prospects' level of knowledge and interest in what you sell (and therefore how to approach them and with that message).

- Keep from losing prospects by bombarding them with too much information too early or attempting to hard sell them (this is why experts often refer to moving leads through the funnel as the "nurturing" process).

- Determine what type and frequency of campaign may be needed to spark interest depending on a prospect's position in the funnel.

- Ensure a common language is fostered and reinforced throughout the funnel to reinforce branding.

I'd love to tell you that sales funnels have become more simplified over the years, but in reality, they have only grown more complex, mainly due to the increase in digital channels and the way consumer behavior is constantly evolving. When it comes to getting the most out of your sales funnel, one thing is certain: "Set it and forget it" isn't going to get the results you want. That is why the best sales funnels are built through analytics:

> **ANALYTICS (NOUN):**
> A way to compute data that highlights meaningful patterns, answers key business questions, uncovers relationships, and predicts outcomes that help automate future decisions.

According to a Salesforce.com report, nearly 70 percent of sales teams say they now regularly use data insights on sales, customers, and prospects to constantly adjust their funnels and keep the nurturing process healthy and flowing.

Later on in the chapter, you'll learn about *key performance indicators* (KPIs) based on numbers called *critical drivers* that can help show you why a business may be thriving or simply surviving. These numbers will become instrumental in the analytics process as you develop and refine your sales funnel.

If you want to run a thriving business with minimal time commitment, get used to crunching numbers, because a healthy sales funnel lives and dies by the numbers.

Business Fundamental #3: Fulfillment
The ability to deliver your product or service.

With today's cutthroat competition, the product or service you supply must be superior, and the way you deliver must be exceptional. Amazon Prime's unprecedented order fulfillment speed and accuracy changed the standards for fulfillment across the board, particularly for tangible products. Also consider online reviews and word of mouth.

People can almost instantly evaluate whether a product or service is valuable or worth the investment in our digital world.

You should be striving to be the best at what you do. In other words, your goal is to create the most value for people when they receive your product or service. Here are the differences in fulfillment processes between a survival-minded business and a thriving business.

Survival Fulfillment:
A surviving business uses a fulfillment process that is too expensive for both the owner and customers. If the fulfillment is "cheap," that cheapness comes at a cost (in the form of subpar, slow, or unreliable deliveries and more). Survival fulfillment represents a whole slew of frustrations, causes repeat sales to be lost, and lowers customer retention. The bottom line is most solo-preneurs (whose business owns them) spend 90 percent of their time dealing with fulfillment instead of marketing and selling.

Thriving Fulfillment:
A prosperous fulfillment process has a premium product or service delivered at a price that gives you a healthy margin. This results in both excess cash and time. The fulfillment of a service or electronic product is seamless and polished. Physical products are delivered with care and in a way that shows how valuable you view both the product and customer. Communication is constant throughout the entire fulfillment process.

The Three Fundamentals in Action

Physical Product: Bicycle Shop

A new bicycle shop chooses to market to its potential customers through newspaper ads, online ads, social media marketing, and

Groupon. The *marketing* theme is to educate customers on the difference between buying a bike at a big box store versus their shop (the experience, the service, and more). This approach allows them to target their demographic quickly and weed out those who would not be a good fit.

Coupons and specials bring people in the door and to their online shop. The quality, selection, craftsmanship, and service offered are what make the *sale*. Also, the shop only hires employees who are passionate about outdoor exercise and cycling. *Fulfillment* occurs immediately upon purchase. If there is a custom order, the shop stays in regular contact with the customer. It informs them systematically exactly when their custom order will arrive. They schedule a particular date and time for the customer to come to pick up their new purchase.

Service as the Product: Law Firm

A law firm chooses to actively *market* their services via television, radio, billboards, online, and social media marketing. They also employ a referral program where existing clients are compensated with complimentary hours or other services for providing the firm with qualified referrals. Their marketing goal is to inform the surrounding area that the firm specializes in injury law. They also focus on customers who may not have sufficient funds to pay hefty retainer fees.

When a lawyer meets with a potential client, that lawyer listens intently and shares success stories related to that potential client's own issues. Once the client agrees to be represented by the firm, the *sale has been made*. But the transaction is far from complete. *Fulfillment* occurs when the lawyer spends his or her time and expertise providing the agreed-upon legal service and delivers exceptional results to the client.

As you can see, successfully executing the three fundamentals means that both a business and their customer walk away from a transaction feeling like they won. It should be a mutually beneficial experience that all parties involved would be more than willing to have again.

THE THREE FUNDAMENTALS OF BUSINESS

	SURVIVING BUSINESS	THRIVING BUSINESS
MARKETING	Not enough leads	Endless pipeline of leads
SELLING	Difficult sales conversions	Easy sales conversions
FULFILLMENT	Time-intensive, inefficient	Outsourced, efficient

Once you begin evaluating a potentially thriving business and developing marketing, sales, and fulfillment processes, that is excellent progress. Next, your potential business must pass the "thriving business" test by meeting five standards for selection.

 How to Choose:
The Five Standards for Selecting a Winning Business

There are five standards that every winning business possesses. If you adhere to these five standards, you'll find that successful entrepreneurship is much easier than you think. You'll also have a higher likelihood of success. Here is a brief summary before we dive into each one:

1. *Profits.* Look for profit margins of 25 percent or greater.

2. *Leads.* Ensure that you can procure abundant lead sources.

3. *Simplicity.* The business model must be stunningly simple.

4. *Delegation.* Operations must be easily delegated to others.

5. *Customer Focus.* Your passion should be for the customer, not the product.

Standard #1: Large Profit Margins

Select a business with a minimum of a 25 percent profit margin.

Most small businesses today simply aren't profitable enough. In fact, as many as 86 percent of all business owners net less than $100,000 per year. The problem could be what they sell, or the problem could be the inherent expenses in selling the product or service. My rule of thumb to avoid a disappointing business venture is to strive for a 25 percent profit margin or more.

At the end of the week, month, and year, the profit margin is the amount of dollars that will find its way into your pocket. That is why you need to know this number and protect it fiercely. And stay away from any and all businesses that don't deliver my bare minimum standard of 25 percent net margin.

While it may be true that giant companies like Walmart, Target, and Ford bring in a scant 3.9 to 5.2 percent net profit margin, you can't afford such small numbers as a sole proprietor. It would require such *enormous* gross revenue that it won't be worth your time or energy.

Survival Profit Margins:

Most businesses run on a 10 percent margin (some experts claim it's even smaller than that, possibly closer to 7 percent). That means they keep a dime or less for every dollar they collect. That also means they have to do a million dollars' worth of business just to net $100,000. This profit margin is too low because the numbers are stacked against them.

Thriving Profit Margins:

A winning business has a minimum of a 25 percent profit margin. Make this your minimum standard before even considering a business venture. You will automatically make two to three times more profit than a typical company.

GOOD TO KNOW
PROFIT MARGIN FORMULA

$$\frac{Profit}{Revenue} \times 100 = \text{Profit Margin (as a percentage)}$$

Profit Margin in Action: Product

Product Revenue: The payment received for selling the product
- Retail sales price: **$200 revenue**

Product Expenses: The cost of selling your product
(portioned out per product sold)
- Product cost: $80 *(cost to acquire the product wholesale)*
- Ad costs and sales commissions: $40
  (paid to generate leads and move lead through the sales funnel)

- Shipping and handling: $20

  (fulfillment cost to send the product to customer)
- Total expenses: $80 + $40 + 20 = **$140 expenses**

Product Profit Margin: Percentage that represents your net profit after expenses

- Profit: $200 revenue – $140 expenses =

  $60 profit netted from the sale
- Profit margin: $60 profit / $200 revenue x 100 =

  30% profit margin (percent of revenue you get to keep)

Profit Margin in Action: Service

Service Revenue: The payment received for selling the service

- Service sales price: **$1,000 revenue**

Service Expenses: The cost of selling your service *(portioned out per service sold)*

- Labor cost (10 hours at $30/hour): $300

  (money paid to service provider)
- Hard costs: $150

  (cost of supplies needed to provide the service)
- Ad costs and sales commissions: $200

  (paid to generate leads and move lead through the sales funnel)
- Total expenses: $300 + $150 + $200 = **$650 expenses**

Service Profit Margin: Percentage that represents your net profit after expenses

- Profit: $1,000 revenue – $650 expenses =

  $350 profit netted from the sale
- Profit margin: $350 profit / $1000 revenue x 100 =

  35% profit margin (percent of revenue you get to keep)

The most obvious way to tank profit margin is to operate with far too high expenses to generate good percentages. Alternatively, you may be offering your goods or services for too little. Since both of the profit margins in the examples above are well above 25 percent, they pass the profit margin test. So, we can continue to the second standard in our list.

Standard #2: Abundant Lead Sources
Select a business with an abundance of leads.

A business becomes a business by offering something that people want to buy. Without the people in that scenario, you certainly do not have a business. At best, you have a costly hobby. The hallmark of a good business venture is leads are easy to acquire at a reasonable cost.

Survival Lead Sources:
Most businesses not only operate on a small margin, but they also lack an adequate supply of leads. This leaves them struggling to stoke that "profit fire" in wet conditions *and* with the wrong supplies. A business without leads simply won't be in business for long. Never, and I mean *never*, consider a business that struggles for adequate lead sources.

Thriving Lead Sources:
A winning business has an abundance of qualified free or inexpensive leads. You should be swimming in leads at all times, or at least have a plan for gaining more.

DEVIL'S ADVOCATE

"But Kris, how do I find leads for my business?"

Let me just go ahead and save you a ton of time and money. If you do not know the answer to this question, do not consider it as a serious business option. You should never be enticed by a brilliant product or service if you will not be able to find or purchase an abundant source of leads.

Many people mistakenly think that the key to business is selling a product or service they personally love or use. I don't entirely disagree with that, but I think it's actually an inferior way to pick a business. What if your biggest passion in life is making SpongeBob-themed quilts for horses? Is there an abundant and never-ending supply of free leads out there for this product? Maybe, maybe not. But you better find out before you set up shop and start buying reams of yellow yarn.

Standard #3: Simple Business Model
Select a business that is simple enough for others to run.

A principle in philosophy and science known as *Occam's Razor* states that the most uncomplicated way to do something is usually the right way. I live my life according to this principle. If a business model (including how you sell a product, how you make money, and how you interact with your customers) is too convoluted, it doesn't 100 percent guarantee failure. But it certainly guarantees a lifetime of frustration.

Survival Business Model:

Most businesses have a complicated business model, and what's the saying? *If something can go wrong, it will.* One of my business mentors, Tony Robbins, taught me that complexity is the enemy of execution and ultimate success. While there are plenty of examples of complex businesses renowned for their success, I'm not here to show you how to build a billion-dollar tech company with a massive infrastructure. I'm here to show you ways to identify multiple simple-but-profitable businesses that don't require sleepless nights or overtime. Suppose the business involves complex technology or pioneering (as in creating something that's never been done before). In that case, this is a huge red flag.

Pioneers and trailblazers learn the hard way.

Thriving Business Model:

Thriving businesses look at innovating or improving upon *existing* ideas and making them better rather than creating something brand new. If the goal is to ultimately have a business run itself, then you also need something duplicatable. Businesses that are the most duplicatable are so simple that you could bring virtually anyone in to help you run it. The business model would make sense to them after only a brief explanation. Striving for simplicity is the fastest path to preserving your time while making excellent money on hefty profit margins.

"Complexity is the enemy of execution."
—Tony Robbins

Standard #4: Operations Easily Delegated
Select a business where you can delegate most tasks.

Most business owners will tell you (along with some eye rolls and a few deep sighs) that fulfillment requires a majority of their time. In other words, the amount of time that it takes to market and sell a product is usually much less than the time that it takes to fulfill. So, how do you keep from doing it all yourself? You delegate!

Survival Delegation:
Because most businesses operate with insufficient profit margins (and therefore can't afford any hires), owners often become the lead or possibly the lone workhorses in their companies. This means they end up working harder than everyone else for the least amount of pay—and, more critically, for a nearly complete loss of their time. The end result is the business ends up owning them.

Thriving Delegation:
If you want something done right, don't do it yourself. Hire other people. Just because you *can* do it doesn't mean you *should*. Doing it all yourself puts you at risk of building your life around your business instead of building your business around your life. A winning business allows you to pass along fulfillment to others and preserve your time. Once you have procedures for delegating fulfillment, your next goal is to delegate marketing and selling duties.

The happiest businesspeople I know live to delegate, but it's not a skill that everyone naturally possesses. **The goal is to own successful companies, not operate successful companies—that is, unless you are prepared to limit your potential.**

If you struggle to trust others and distribute responsibilities, start the soul-searching process now and figure out how to let your guard down enough to let others help you. It's the only way to reclaim more of your time and still run a successful business or side hustle.

You own the business, not the other way around.

Standard #5: Customer Focus

Select a business where the passion is for the customer, not the product itself.
Beware of the draw of doing your "passion" for a living. The most successful business owners fall in love with providing an outstanding customer experience rather than being enamored with their own products or services. It can be a hard distinction to make, I'll admit. This is because there are three primary roles within most businesses: 1) the owner, 2) the manager, and 3) the artist/specialist who creates or curates the product or service.

The key is to ensure that you are not playing all three roles.

 Survival Passion:
Most businesses are conceived by people who have such a passion for a particular product or service that they turn it into a living. While passion can be a massive benefit to a business, it can also be a curse. A misplaced passion for products and services over the customer will ultimately trap you in a never-ending rat race you cannot escape (actually, it isn't never-ending—it usually ends with your demise and the death of your business ownership dreams). You could be bleeding money but find it impossible to give up on your dream because your passion for the product has clouded your judgment.

Thriving Passion:

A winning business creates value for the client and allows you, the business owner, to fall in love with the customer and not the product itself. Feel free to let your passion be part of your business, as long as you don't spend more than the first few months playing the artist or manager role. Otherwise, you're at risk of getting "stuck" in the business's emotion and lose sight of the bottom line and what it takes to increase it—happy customers.

THE FIVE STANDARDS OF BUSINESS SELECTION

	SURVIVING BUSINESS	THRIVING BUSINESS
ROBUST PROFIT MARGINS	Averages a paltry 10 percent profit margin	Aims for a minimum of a 25 percent profit margin
ABUNDANT LEAD SOURCES	Lacks an adequate supply of leads	Has an abundance of qualified leads
SIMPLE BUSINESS MODEL	Has a complicated business model that is easy to mess up	Is duplicatable and can run itself
EASILY DELEGATED OPERATIONS	Can't hire out fulfillment and takes up all your time	Hires someone else to handle fulfillment and preserve time
PASSION FOR THE CUSTOMER	Has such passion for products and services that the owner plays the roles of artist and manager. Emotion ruins the business.	Creates value for the client rather than placing all emphasis on the product.

Adhering to my five standards of a thriving business will protect you from making the most common mistakes that destroy many other ventures. These standards allow you to remain laser-focused on being a *business owner* (low time commitment) instead of a *business operator* (full-time commitment).

When I identify a business that meets all five standards, I move into the rapid launch phase to ultimately determine whether it will be a winner in the long run.

 ## 3 How To Start:
The Four Launch Phases of a Successful Business

Once you have a potential business, the next step is to put that business through four launch phases: 1) Evaluate, 2) Experiment, 3) Optimize, and 4) Hand-off. Nine out of every 10 concepts will never meet my high standards. I actually enjoy shooting down ideas when they are missing even one of these criteria. Doing so will save you an untold amount of time, frustration, and money investing in the wrong business.

Phase 1: Evaluate

Phase 1 involves ensuring that the business can meet the three fundamental criteria and the five standards for selection. You must be able to answer yes to the following questions:

Three Fundamentals of Business

1. **Marketing:** Does the business have a way to acquire an endless supply of leads?

2. **Selling:** Does the business have a product or service in high demand?

3. *Fulfillment:* Does the business have a premium offering that can be delivered at a price that maintains a healthy margin?

Five Standards for Selection

1. *Profit Margin:* Does the business have a profit margin of at least 25 percent?

2. *Abundant Leads:* Does the business have an abundance of free or inexpensive leads?

3. *Simplistic:* Can the business run itself, and is it duplicatable?

4. *Delegable:* Does the business allow me to hire others to do fulfillment?

5. *Proper Passion:* Does the business create value for the client and place their needs above the product?

How does your potential business idea stack up?

If you can respond yes to all EIGHT of the above questions, then proceed to the second phase.

Phase 2: Experiment

Never obligate yourself long-term to a business unless you can test it before formally committing. Most simple business ideas can be tested and proven or disproven within 30 days. Maybe you think 30 days isn't long enough to determine whether a business will be a success. In my experience, 30 days is long enough to spot red flags. During that time, you can get a glimpse of what the process will entail from a profit margin and time commitment standpoint.

So, how does this experiment work?

1. First, select a revenue goal and corresponding net profit margin that you determine is achievable in the next 30 days.

2. Then, work as diligently as you can for a month to hit that goal.

3. Finally, if you have not reached 50 percent of that goal at the end of the 30 days, scrap the business idea.

It's as simple as that. If the business is a good idea, you should see swift results. Don't delude yourself into believing that something excessively difficult will become easy with time. This is a recipe for massive disappointment.

Don't waste years of your life and untold dollars on a business that can't generate enough profits to free up your time. Wait as long as it takes to find a concept that confidently meets these standards. I don't care how long it takes to find one. Find the next opportunity and start the evaluation process all over again.

If your business idea passes the experiment phase, proceed to the third phase.

"Measurement is the first step that leads to control and eventually to improvement. If you can't measure something, you can't understand it. If you can't understand it, you can't control it. If you can't control it, you can't improve it." —H. James Harrington

Phase 3: Optimize

By now, you have thoroughly vetted your idea according to established business standards and conducted a successful 30-day experiment. Now it's time to evaluate the business by documenting what works. Phase 3 is a 90-day optimization process that starts with measuring and reporting to determine whether this business is designed to win or sputter out somewhere down the line. The purpose of the optimization phase is to identify three fundamental elements you need to know before you can successfully delegate any part of your business to someone else: 1) key performance indicators, or KPIs, 2) critical drivers, and 3) standard operating procedures, or SOPs.

Element 1:
Key Performance Indicators (KPIs)

KPIs are measurable values that demonstrate how effectively a company is achieving key business objectives. These are the weekly numbers that matter in *any* business. There are literally hundreds of potential KPIs that you may eventually want to consider. Still, there are only three KPI *categories* that really matter (and they just so happen to be the same as our three business fundamentals): marketing, sales, and fulfillment.

Your KPIs are the best tools to determine whether you are on track to hit your target revenue and net profit margin. In the beginning, you will use KPIs to prove or disprove that the business will allow you to hit revenue and margin goals.

In other words, KPIs will reveal if your business can pay all of its expenses and still net at least 25 percent without you working full time.

Yes, it may feel like there are a million things to track. Regardless, ultimately just a handful of key performance indicators are all you really need to reveal a business' potential. The KPIs you follow during the 90-day optimization period should be able to answer the following three questions:

1. How many leads am I generating?

2. What percentage of those leads are converting into sales?

3. How satisfied are my customers after both the sale and fulfillment processes are complete?

These three questions are just the beginning—but they will help get you started tracking the correct information. In addition to answering these three questions, always calculate revenue and net profit margin to determine whether or not your business is on target at the end of each week.

Element 2:
Critical Drivers

Critical drivers measure the activities your team does daily to produce your weekly KPIs. In other words:

A critical driver is a cause, and the KPI is the effect.

Obviously, a wide range of factors impacts the performance of your business. The secret is to focus on a handful of critical drivers that: 1) are specific and measurable, 2) will accurately reflect business progress and performance, and 3) can be compared to those from previous periods.

To establish which critical drivers to track, ask yourself:

- What drives my sales figures?

- How many leads do I get daily?

- What is my daily conversion rate?

- What is my daily number of transactions?

- What factors drive costs (ex: labor, wholesale pricing)?

If you're not getting the results you want according to your KPIs, look at your business activities or critical drivers. This will help you understand whether you're tracking the most revealing activities.

You should track between three and five critical drivers (daily activities) for every employee working in the business. This is how you gather the measurements needed to calculate weekly KPIs. Here are a few examples of critical drivers:

- The number of leads.

- The number of sales calls.

- The number of customers.

After you record these daily drivers, you then have the raw materials (the numbers) you need to calculate key performance indicators (KPIs) such as:

- How much revenue did I generate this week (gross revenue)?

- What is our profit margin after expenses (net profit margin)?

The process of tracking critical drivers and using them to calculate KPIs may seem intimidating. Baby steps are key here. Just look at one number at a time. Go back to my five criteria and start from there.

What are the basic costs of running the business, and what daily numbers does your business generate? And how does that all affect how much money you can successfully reinvest into the vehicles that power your financial freedom blueprint?

Element 3:
Standard Operating Procedures (SOPs)

Standard Operating Procedures or SOPs are a set of step-by-step instructions compiled by an organization to help workers carry out routine operations. You could probably write an entire book about SOPs, but I'll just say this:

> *If you or anyone else who works for you regularly performs a step in your business, write down the step's proper execution process and standardize it. This is a critical and necessary step in the delegating process that will enable you to free your time.*

Think of an SOP as a manual for how people perform work within your business. The most efficient way to create your SOPs is to make employees responsible for creating the SOPs that produce the recorded results in their particular role.

SOPs make it *so* much easier to onboard new employees. Instead of holding their hand throughout the training process, you can provide them with a step-by-step manual that explains the most efficient way to perform duties. As long as you hire right by bringing in people who are fast learners and teachable, SOPs make hiring and training a more hands-off endeavor than most business owners believe it can be.

Create an SOP for the three fundamental areas (marketing, selling, and fulfillment) and document each process. For example:

- *Marketing*—What is the precise process for generating leads? What do you do with a lead once it enters the pipeline?

- *Selling*—How do you approach sales? Is it a hands-off or involved process?

- *Fulfillment*—How do you track orders to make sure you are over-delivering on promised value?

Once you document SOPs and track KPIs from the critical driver data you regularly collect, you empower the business to become a well-oiled machine that requires only the most minor of weekly adjustments.

If it's not already glaringly obvious, the key to running a hands-off business that generates massive income is the proper *groundwork*. This plan is not for the lazy. You need to be diligent and detailed for several months. But think of the long-term payoff! How much are you willing to invest for a few months to enjoy a lifetime of wealth and time freedom?

THE MATH MAKES IT ALL WORTHWHILE

Let's say you invest $100 in total expenses per sale for a service that sells for $200. By netting $100 for every sale you make, that creates a 50 percent profit margin.

Now, let's say you acquire 100 new customers in 30 days (that's just over three customers a day, which, at that price point, should frankly be like shooting fish in a barrel with the right lead generation system and sales funnel).

You spend $100 fixed cost per sale x 100 customers = $10,000 investment.

You collected $200 gross revenue x 100 customers = $20,000 monthly gross revenue.

So, let's do the ROI on that:

$$\frac{20,000 \ (earnings)}{10,000 \ (investment)} \times 100 = 200 \ percent \ ROI$$

This is triple-digit ROI in a *single month*. In one month! Imagine the compounding effects of this kind of return! *This* is why your net profit margin matters so much. So, find the numbers that make it worth all the research and initial investment or don't bother.

Phase 4: The Hand-off

You found an exciting business idea and vetted it. You ran an experiment and determined the business can produce at least 50 percent of expected results. For 90 days, you optimized the business idea and determined KPIs, critical drivers, and SOPs.

It has been an intense four or so months, I realize. But the hard work is truly almost over—and that's the beauty of this process! The time has now come for you to hand it off to someone else after you have ensured that the business has the processes and procedures in place that will produce the same or better revenue and net profit margins.

You put in some work (mostly in the form of research and testing) on the front end for a few short months. After that, the amount of time you spend will be up to you. I am willing to part with up to 20 percent of a business' profits for someone else to take on 95 percent of the workload and therefore free up my time.

The goal with such an involved evaluation process is to ensure that you can hand off the business for other people to run so you can enjoy life and all of its blessings!

After you've successfully been through the 120-day process and completed the hand-off, you will simply have weekly meetings with the operator/manager to review and ensure the KPIs are improving as the business is growing.

WARNING!

The biggest mistake a business owner makes is claiming that working in their own company will allow them to create higher profit margins. *Don't do it*. Your time is too valuable to be tied to a new job when the original goal was to create freedom.

Remember, you are looking for a minimum 25 percent margin after paying all positions, including the job you may be doing within the business. This makes it easier to still enjoy a healthy profit margin while freeing your time for your next project.

Now *that's* freedom.

Time to Rinse and Repeat

Every business has its own natural "market cap." So, when you feel your time is no longer being financially rewarded by spending more time in the business, it may be time to do it all over again with a new thriving business idea.

Yes, you can repeat this process and start another business (and yet another income stream). That is how you generate *seismic* returns that enable you to achieve complete financial freedom in a few years instead of a few decades.

> ### MARKET CAPITALIZATION (NOUN):
>
> Market capitalization, or market cap, refers to the total market value of a business. The term is usually reserved for companies that are actively traded in the stock market. But in reality, every company has a natural cap or ceiling they reach, beyond which it would take too much time, money, or effort to increase. When you consistently track KPIs, the market cap of your business cap should naturally reveal itself.
>
> It's just the ebbs and flows of trade and supply and demand.

As you repeat this process, you'll develop more income streams. More importantly, every time you successfully complete this process, you will generate more income to place into your reserve vehicle to fuel your other investments.

This is how you take maximum advantage of compounding interest.

Generating an active income through a minimal-time-commitment business allows you to exponentially increase your investment potential. With each active income stream created:

- You are placing more money into your S.W.A.N. (Sleep Well At Night) account for greater peace of mind.

- You are putting more money into your passive real estate and stock market investments, producing double-digit and triple-digit ROIs.

- You are also enabling your reserve vehicle to fuel even more active streams of income with impressive net profit margins.

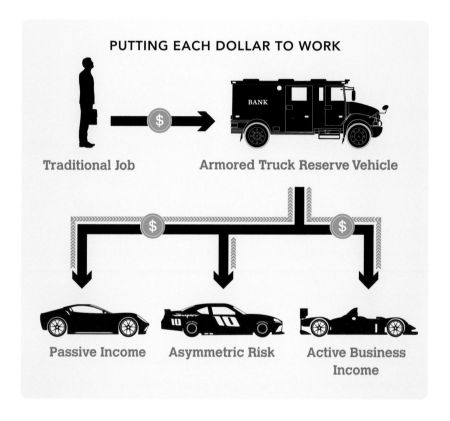

Fast forward a few months or years down the road, and your whole outlook on savings, investments, retirement, and the future itself will have completely transformed. You'll think back on the early days when you thought it was "impossible" to stash 20 percent of your income away, and you'll want to write a letter to that older version of you:

Dear Past Me,

Hang in there! You are doing an incredible job. I know the 20 per-cent feels so hard, but it doesn't stay hard. You are about to step into complete financial freedom! I'm proud of you and can't wait for you to see just how good it's going to get.

Sincerely,

Future me

Take It From Trent

Have you been wondering how things turned out for my forensically-minded friend, Trent?

Well, I'm happy to report that he followed my advice and kept his promise by following my three simple rules. Because of that, he was able to take control of his own destiny. Here is what happened to Trent, in his own words:

> *"Whether you're one of Kris's best friends or someone he just met, you will discover that his willingness to help people is sincere. Kris asked me if I was willing to try something different, something you don't hear from most people. He believed I had what it took, and I trusted that he knew what he was talking about.*
>
> *Kris explained a commonly overlooked way to generate leads online. I was fortunate that I had not lost my job yet, but I knew I couldn't keep doing it for much longer. And if I didn't get fired, I'd quit.*
>
> *So, in the beginning, I committed to spending up to two-and-a-half hours a day before and after work following up on the leads (primarily from Facebook). I started booking jobs, and within the*

first 30 days, I booked enough work to earn $9,100 in commission. The first and second weeks were slow, and I started to get frustrated, but I trusted the process, and weeks three and four picked up momentum."

Trent has since taken this opportunity a step further than most people do. He hired someone to help him generate and track leads. Trent also hired a social media marketing firm to optimize and run variations of his Facebook ads. Then he expanded his market reach across the United States. After testing his new ads for six weeks, he kept the high-performing ones and scrapped the duds.

My friend has taken a very systematic approach to making this side hustle a long-term, lucrative active income stream, and I couldn't be prouder. Trent now expects his "side hustle" (that enabled him to quit his old job) to consistently bring in from $8,000 to $12,000 a month, with a time investment of just 30 minutes to an hour a day.

The fascinating part is he started as a business operator and became a business owner within a few months. Now, he delegates others to do tasks that he doesn't want to do or doesn't have time to do. Trent's advice:

"If you're not willing to take a risk and potentially lose for the first couple of months, then don't do it. But if you're willing to put yourself out there and are able to bounce back from rejection (because rejection is inevitable when you own a business), then you can do this. In fact, anyone can! You just have to decide to be bold and have confidence."

Trent went far beyond replacing his income and made enough money to leave his job and step into financial freedom. Four-digit ROI through an active income that generates at least a 25 percent margin can be *the* game-changer. Trent now has multiple income streams, and it has changed his lifestyle, goals, and overall financial direction.

Looking for a thriving business or side hustle that meets my five high standards?

I have several I'd like to tell you more about.

I'm talking about ventures requiring minimal time after the evaluation period. These businesses grant you the freedom to continue working your day job if you want and saying goodbye to it forever if you don't.

If you want to learn about my favorite business opportunity, which meets my thriving business standards (and can generate up to seven figures of active income in today's market), check out my Master Class at **KrisKrohn.com/Business**.

Now that you're saving and investing like never before, you also have more options than ever before. So, let's shift gears and accelerate into our financial freedom blueprint's fifth and final stage: infinite ROI through strategic partnerships.

CHAPTER EIGHT CHECKPOINT

1. Traditional business goals leave out a critical ingredient—to create both profit and value without sacrificing too much of your valuable time.

2. There are three fundamentals of business required to take your venture from surviving to thriving. You must have a plan for: 1) marketing, 2) selling, and 3) fulfillment.

3. Every thriving business must meet five criteria for selection: 1) high-profit margins, 2) an abundance of leads, 3) a simple business model, 4) delegable processes, and 5) a customer-focused passion.

4. To rapidly launch a thriving business, utilize the four launch phases: 1) evaluate, 2) experiment, 3) optimize, and 4) outsource.

5. Key performance indicators (KPIs) are how you, the business owner, meaningfully interpret the numbers that matter in any business.

6. Creating standard operating procedures (SOPs) in all three of the fundamental areas of business will prepare you to successfully hand operations over to someone else after the evaluation period. This ensures you remain the owner and not the operator.

No one can
whistle a symphony.
It takes a whole orchestra
to play it.

NINE

YOUR STRATEGIC PARTNERSHIP VEHICLE

Infinite ROI

MY PHONE RANG on a Monday morning, and I heard my father-in-law Matt's voice. We exchanged pleasantries, and I asked him how his trip had been since I knew he and my mother-in-law had just returned from celebrating their anniversary.

But I could tell he didn't want to talk about his vacation. He cut right to the chase. "Can you tell me about the real estate you've been buying?"

The question immediately put me on edge. Not because I didn't enjoy discussing real estate. It was because I believed Matt thought I was nuts for buying houses. A few years before, I had to look him in the eyes and tell him I dropped out of pre-med. Then, I went and bought a house in a college town with no degree and no declared major.

Why would his son-in-law do that?

To Matt and to the rest of the known universe, you buy a house only once you're "sure." You're *sure* of where you want to live and raise your family. You're *sure* you've got the right career that can cover the mortgage.

But the thing is, I wasn't sure about anything.

A little while later, when I bought my second house, he was even more confused. *What young married couple needs two properties unless they're headed for a divorce?*

When I bought my third house, no doubt he concluded that I'd completely lost my mind. I wasn't following the plan he thought would make his daughter safe and secure. As a young man, Matt had gotten his undergrad in business and went back for his MBA, and now he worked for a successful company.

That is the model you use to provide for a family—right?

I seemed to be following a starkly different model. If you'd asked me what that model was at the time, I'm sure I appeared as directionless as a bag in the wind. I was still figuring it all out myself, but I knew I was onto something.

Given all of this, my nervousness about Matt asking real estate questions is probably more understandable. But I kept my cool, responded with a matter-of-factness, and listened to what he had to say, trying to read between the lines.

It didn't take long to figure out what was going on.

First, he wanted to know the difference between the sale price and the value of the homes I bought. He also wanted to know how much I was netting on rent. As he continued, I could have sworn I heard the faint scribbling of a pen and some tip-tapping on a calculator.

At one point, he even asked me my thoughts on traditional investment vehicles like his 401(k). I didn't hold back.

He let it all sink in, and then there was a silence for a moment before he continued. "So, what's your next move, Kris?"

I proceeded to tell him about a fourth property I had my eye on and how much cash flow it would generate (if I could just figure out how to fund it).

"How much do you need?" he asked.

I told Matt I needed $20,000, and his next question caught me entirely off guard. "How about I put up the money? You do all the work, and then when it's done, we split the profits 50/50."

In that instant, I felt an insane rush of adrenaline. Something had just clicked.

My father-in-law had suddenly unlocked the opportunity that would ultimately create millions of dollars for me and scores of future business partners. The realization hit me like a ton of bricks that I no longer needed my *own* money to make money in real estate.

Why use my own money when I could use someone else's?

Infinite Business Partners

Before I even graduated from BYU, Matt and I had already purchased nine homes together. I remember one day during my last semester of college, the professor had gone off on a tangent about something, and it gave my mind a little time to wander.

> *How had I gotten so lucky to have a father-in-law who had money saved in traditional retirement vehicles? Then this same father-in-law* also *trusted me enough to help him use his savings to create better returns?*

My next thought after that was: *Where can I sign up to get more fathers-in-law?* But I didn't need more in-laws. What I really needed was a way to consistently duplicate this type of partnership.

One day shortly after, it dawned on me that several people in my circle had kept regular tabs on my real estate success. So, I made a shortlist of those who I thought might be more naturally interested in partnering with me. This sounds like the start of a corny joke, but my list included:

1. A dentist.

2. A corporate executive.

3. An optometrist.

4. A small business owner.

I decided to call all four and offer to take each one to lunch. During each lunch meeting, I proposed a partnership like the one I had with my father-in-law. I didn't show up empty-handed—I had taken the time to create a professional-looking portfolio that included all of my properties, and I proceeded to share:

- The results of my last 10 real estate purchases.

- The cash flow received from each property.

- The discount I was receiving when I bought the properties.

- The ROI earned on each, as well as the compounding ROI on all properties and my re-investments.

Every one of them had the same reaction as my father-in-law. It was something like, *"Where has this been my whole life?"* and *"Whoa, this kid is kicking the trash out of my retirement plans!"*

Each lunch appointment ended the same way. We excitedly shook hands as I welcomed them as my newest business partner. Our agreements had a simple structure (remember Occam's Razor):

1. They would put up the money as the *passive* partner.

2. I would do all the work as the *active* partner.

3. After they recouped the initial investment, we split the profits.

It didn't take me long to realize that as long as my real estate investments performed well, I could take on as many partners as needed. The end result would be to create a massive hoard of properties, all made possible through the power of other people's resources.

Infinite ROI Unlocked

I may have been terrible at chemistry (which was why I dropped pre-med), but I was *great* at statistics, as it turns out. This worked out well since Statistics 101 at BYU was designed as a "weed-out" course. Let me tell you what a weed-out course is. It's basically a class designed to fail those who have no business pursuing that subject any further. And it simultaneously puts a spotlight on the rock stars.

The statistics professor told us on the first day of class: "My job is to fail 90 percent of you." But I wasn't scared for a minute. I didn't even have to study. It all came naturally to me like I'd been born spewing statistics. When it came time for the final exam, I absolutely destroyed the curve, much to the dismay of the rest of my class. My final grade for the course was an A+ (I actually got a 113), while my classmates mainly got Ds.

I had finally discovered my passion for numbers. But you don't have to be a statistician to appreciate what I'm about to share with you.

Through a few simple calculations, I will explain the power of *your money* invested into real estate compared to the power of *other people's money* invested into real estate. We'll use nice, round numbers to keep things simple, but this concept works no matter how simple or complex the deal:

Example A. Your Money at Work
Traditional ROI

Let's say you saved $40,000 and invested it as a 20 percent down payment for a property. Then, you sold the house four years later and made your initial $40,000 back along with an additional $40,000 profit.

You doubled your money over four years! But don't take my word for it. Let's do the math.

First, calculate total ROI and then annual ROI:

TOTAL ROI ON YOUR MONEY

$$\frac{40{,}000 \text{ gain}}{40{,}000 \text{ investment}} = 1 \times 100 = 100 \text{ percent total ROI}$$

ANNUAL ROI ON YOUR MONEY

$$\frac{100\% \text{ total ROI}}{4 \text{ years}} = 25 \text{ percent annual ROI}$$

Making 25 percent on your investment every year for a total of 100 percent return on investment is already impressive. But I've done that deal thousands of times. So, let's get to the exciting part.

Example B. Your Partner's Money at Work
Infinite ROI

Assume you do the exact same real estate deal, but, this time, your partner provides the $40,000 for the initial investment. You and your team do all of the work. Four years later, your partner gets his $40,000 initial investment back upon the sale of the property.

But there's also the matter of that $40,000 profit. Your partner gets $20,000, and you get $20,000.

Let's check out your partner's ROI first:

Your partner invests $40,000 and receives a total of $60,000 back (original investment of $40,000 + $20,000 in profits).

TOTAL ROI FOR YOUR PARTNER

$$\frac{20{,}000 \text{ gain}}{40{,}000 \text{ investment}} = .5 \times 100 = 50 \text{ percent total ROI}$$

ANNUAL ROI FOR YOUR PARTNER

$$\frac{50 \text{ percent total ROI}}{4 \text{ years}} = 12.5 \text{ percent annual ROI}$$

A 12.5 percent ROI would make almost any investor (especially one who has been using society's retirement vehicles) thrilled!

But what about *your* results? You made $20,000 but invested $0.

What is your ROI?

I know you desperately wanted to do more math, but there is no math to be done here. I call it an "*infinite* ROI" because the results you can expect when leveraging strategic partnerships really are limitless. But in reality, you cannot calculate an answer at all.

A fundamental rule of fractions is that you can't have a zero in the denominator. When you do, the result is undefined. It's an impossible result. In other words:

You have defied the laws of mathematics with your investing brilliance!

You put in no money, but you received $20,000 in profit. That's not even supposed to be possible. And yet it happened. This is profit that my partners and other smart investors turn around and invest right into more real estate.

With a minimum 25 percent ROI over 20 years, that insignificant $50,000 has the potential to become $4.3M compared to what it would likely produce in traditional stock market investments—which is a measly $160,000.

We're talking about 27 times more money.

That is why I call this vehicle your infinite ROI private jet, and it earns its rightful and critical place on the Financial Freedom Roadmap on the following page.

FINANCIAL FREEDOM ROADMAP

① RESERVE
Save 20% of your income in your single-digit ROI account.

Financial Reserve Vehicle
Single-digit ROI

② INVEST
Invest reserves into high ROI vehicles.

③ CONVERT
Create lifestyle cash flow through high ROIs and reinvest.

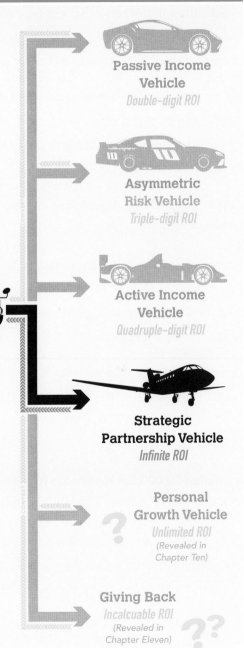

Passive Income Vehicle
Double-digit ROI

Asymmetric Risk Vehicle
Triple-digit ROI

Active Income Vehicle
Quadruple-digit ROI

Strategic Partnership Vehicle
Infinite ROI

Personal Growth Vehicle
Unlimited ROI
(Revealed in Chapter Ten)

Giving Back
Incalcuable ROI
(Revealed in Chapter Eleven)

I love the term "infinite ROI" because it does an excellent job of conveying the closest thing you can get to "pulling money out of thin air." Now, I said earlier in the book that matter cannot be created or destroyed, but only change forms—and that's still true (I may have defied the laws of mathematics, but I'll leave the laws of physics alone).

My intent with the idea of "infinite ROI through strategic partnerships" is to help you let go of limiting beliefs. Just imagine the possibilities that await when you have not only your *own* resources at your disposal, but also the endless resources of *others*.

You're not pulling money out of thin air. You're just helping it change forms.

So, we've established that you can't determine ROI without an initial investment. Therefore, the best possible way to calculate your return when you utilize strategic partnerships is to look at the value or worth of your *time*. For example:

I leverage a team to buy real estate. They do all of the legwork on every part of the deals from start to finish, and I spend maybe 15 minutes of my time on each deal. Five years later, let's say I make $50,000 on the sale of a property.

If I made $50,000 for 15 minutes (or one-quarter of an hour) of work, that equates to making $200,000 an hour.

Guys, I'm really not that special. If my time can be worth $200,000 an hour on a deal, then your time can be highly valuable as well. So, how can you tap into something so powerful?

The magic comes in the "Power of Three."

The Power of Three

Earning double-digit returns in real estate is excellent! Through the act of buying, holding, and selling properties, you can leave the returns of those old investment vehicles in the dust. But earning infinite ROIs through leveraging other people's money? Even better! All you need to get started is to focus on the number *three*.

ZERO ...

Imagine you have a friend with some savings who might be willing to become your real estate partner. The problem is you have no track record and have completed no deals. How is this friend going to respond to your proposal? If they're smart, they'll say no.

ONE ...

Let's assume you've had one successful deal. You certainly can't call that a "track record of success," but at least it's not *nothing*. Still, it could have been luck. But you made good money once, so if you ask this individual whether they want to partner with you. The answer should be no once again—if that friend isn't foolish.

TWO ...

Now let's say you've had two good deals back-to-back. You approach this potential partner, and this time you feel more confident about your odds. The thing is, two is still in the realm of "just got lucky." It could have been a fluke. Sorry, but no dice.

THREE!

Something changes when you have success three times in a row. It now becomes a *pattern*! Patterns are magical. When you meet with this potential partner and tell them about your three successful deals, your friend will get a funny feeling inside. It's something called the *fear of missing out* (often abbreviated as FOMO).

Three is the minimum magic number that makes people want to partner with you. You've found a pattern for manifesting real estate success, as well as success in business, and they want in on it! Successful business owners with a track record of growing companies get investors to back their ideas so they can grow businesses with other people's money.

In order to get the infinite ROI ball rolling, work on developing that track record. What that means to you today is simply this:

> Focus on building an initial portfolio of no fewer than three homes. That is enough of a track record to approach potential partners. Implement the business plan from the previous chapter and work on building a few successful businesses with the kind of KPIs that attract future partners.

Make a plan for saving that will enable you to purchase a minimum of three properties. Do that, and you'll have something impressive to show potential partners. Once you have completed those three deals, you are ready. Review your contact list and reach out to everyone who is:

- 35 years or older.

- Financially conservative.

- Makes an above-average income.

These people are individuals who have likely been:

- Putting money into 401(k)s and IRAs.

- Focusing on paying off their house.

- Setting assets aside for their retirement.

By the time you approach them, there's a solid chance they've grown at least partially disenchanted with their traditional retirement plan. They may have looked at their investment accounts (the ones that are supposed to make them feel warm and snuggly and secure) and wondered why they haven't grown to be more substantial.

Share the three deals you've successfully completed, professionally present the numbers, and walk them step-by-step through the ROIs. There's a high probability they will decide to put up the money for your fourth deal.

If you can find just *one* partner, then with each additional home you buy together, it builds your success track record in real estate investing. The more you add to your track record, the easier it is to get another partner.

Your first partner will be the hardest to acquire, but the second and third will follow suit much more quickly and easily. Before long, you will find yourself on a success path that is much like mine. You'll have the ability to invest in real estate without using any of your own money whatsoever—and it's glorious to step into the power of infinite results.

Action Steps for Creating Infinite Results

I have great news: **This same principle of infinite ROI works in business.** You never have to be restricted by your own wallet again as long as you have some initial track record on an idea with positive duplicatable results.

If you think the numbers with infinite business partners look good on 25 percent ROI real estate deals, then imagine how good they look on businesses with triple- and quadruple-digit ROI potential.

The better you become at doing business, the better your established track record will be. This creates a desire for people to partner with you on your next business venture. Start a new business and generate high net profit margins that enable you to start another business (and then another). After this, I predict many investors will get that FOMO feeling and want a piece of the action.

They say it takes money to make money, and they're right (whoever "they" are). But they never said *whose* money it has to be.

As you build a track record for succeeding in business, you will likewise earn the trust of individuals who will want to partner with you. But none of this can happen without step one! Step one is to save money in your financial reserve vehicle. Step two is to parcel those funds out to your different investments.

As we continue, I am going to ask you to start seeing your track record of success in business and real estate as an asset. We think of time and money as assets, but track record is my most valuable asset that I trade for money and more time.

As each investment vehicle performs, it will generate cash flow to redeposit back into your interest-earning life insurance savings account. And then things really start to pick up the pace.

- The more you *invest*, the more *experience* you get.

- The more *experience* you get, the better your *track record* becomes.

- The better your *track record*, the more *credibility* you build.

- The more *credibility* you build, the more *partners* you attract.

- The more *partners* you attract, the deeper into the land of *infinite returns* you travel.

Before long, the time will come when people with money will seek *you* out for partnership. It's a beautiful thing to defy the rules of mathematics and break the calculator on your way to financial freedom.

And that, my friend, is how you utilize the most potent accelerant to achieving financial freedom sooner rather than later.

"But Kris, I don't want to wait that long before I unlock infinite ROI!"

I don't blame you! Fortunately, it is possible to achieve an infinite ROI without a track record through one shortcut: *Leveraging someone else's track record.*

I recently discovered that many of my clients and social media followers had introduced their friends and family to my real estate investing system. Without even realizing it, they leveraged my personal track record. Many people chose to partner with me simply because of their friends' recommendations.

Given how often this was happening, I launched a program that allows my followers and clients to refer potential partners. If their referral prospect is the right candidate for partnering, I share 50 percent of my ownership.

Why am I doing this? I've already built my wealth. I've also reached a point in my life where I'll never spend another moment worrying about how to provide for my family. So, I choose to give back.

Remember, it doesn't have to be your money, and it also doesn't have to be your track record. Ultimately, you are simply combining resources to make deals happen. My mentor, Tony Robbins, says it best:

"It's not about your resources; it's about your resourcefulness."

I will admit that my style is unconventional. I also know that my approach to earning infinite ROIs is very *maverick* in nature.

MAVERICK (NOUN):

A person who marches to the beat of their own drum. Someone who refuses to adhere to customary rules and standards "just because" it's what is expected.

Visit **KrisKrohn.com/Mavericks** if you'd like to learn more about becoming a Maverick. There, you can download a free copy of the guide I put together to walk you through the process of developing a team of investor partners. This plan works even when you're starting from scratch with no money and no one in your network!

CHAPTER NINE CHECKPOINT

1. People with savings are often willing to supply the investment and be passive investor partners in real estate. At the same time, you invest nothing but your time and expertise. Then you split the profits after they recover their investment.

2. After discovering how strategic partnerships exponentially multiplied my earnings, I reached out to my qualified contacts and presented the opportunity to them. Those with FOMO (fear of missing out) always want in!

3. Your own money at work in real estate can quickly produce double-digit annual returns. However, your ROI on other people's money is infinite (you literally cannot calculate it).

4. Before you can start putting other people's money to work, you need to respect the power of *three*. You need to have at least three successful real estate deals before your partnership offer becomes desirable to investors.

5. Don't forget that step one is to put money into your reserve vehicle before you can start investing and building a track record.

6. If you want to shortcut the "power of three" rule, you must find a way to leverage other successful investors' track records.

WHAT IS MY CUSTOM GAME PLAN FOR GETTING STARTED?

We have reached the end of Part Two! I've got to ask: How are you feeling? Are you excited? Overwhelmed? I've thrown a lot of life-changing information your way, so if you're in a state of information overload, it's totally understandable. The best recommendation is to start taking the action steps as quickly as possible. Here are the pieces you need to formulate your custom game plan:

Destination #1: Set up your reserve. If you haven't set aside any savings, your top priority is to start filling up that armored truck (or add more to it). Determine how much you will set aside and set up a free consultation about your life insurance savings account at: *KrisKrohn.com/CashFlow.*

Destination #2: Get into the real estate game. Real estate is for everyone, no matter where you are today with your savings. To learn from my investment team about building a winning portfolio, visit: *KrisKrohn.com/Portfolio.*

Destination #3: Learn to use asymmetric risk. To take advantage of my research into emerging industries and exciting high-ROI companies and see more of my passive trading strategies, visit: *KrisKrohn.com/Stocks.*

Destination #4: Discover a thriving business. For free access to a quick guide of the top six business opportunities that meet my thriving business standards, visit: *KrisKrohn.com/Business.*

Destination #5: Unlock infinite ROI. If you want to create ROIs that shouldn't even be mathematically possible, it's time to tap into strategic partnerships. To download your guide for the process of developing a team of investor partners, visit: *KrisKrohn.com/Mavericks.*

I've painstakingly detailed the different vehicles designed, with great speed and energy, to get you from a place of worry about the future to a place where you can have it all in the not-so-distant future. In that place, you can leave worry at the door and step fully into abundant living.

CALL TO ACTION! If you would like a complimentary game-plan to examine your current situation and what moves you may want to make next, get in touch with one of my Wealth Coaches. Go here to request one: **KrisKrohn.com/Wealth**.

Now, you could stop now and transform your life through what you've learned in this book. But if you're anything like me, you want more. So, keep reading because we are about to discuss the final integral pieces of the puzzle for creating your dream life and leaving a legacy that lasts beyond your own limited time on this earth.

We have two final vehicles to reveal in the final chapters that deserve their own place on the road map. I wouldn't be here today without them, and I hope you'll digest the information and act, because it will forever change the trajectory of your life.

Are you left wondering whether you can truly achieve financial freedom in five years or less? Well, here's part of that answer:

1. Stash cash into a **single-digit ROI truck**—you're on the road to freedom.

2. Unleash the power of **double-digit ROI**—retire within a decade or more.

3. Master the **triple-digit ROIs** of risk—achieve your goals in years.

4. Unlock **quadruple-digit ROIs**—you go from years to months.

5. Step into **infinite ROIs**—it's no longer a question of "if" but "how fast."

I'll answer the question more fully in the last part of the book. So, if you really want to see, finish last three chapters and find out yourself.

PART THREE

CREATING THE ULTIMATE ROI

For the best
return on your money,
pour your purse
into your head.

BENJAMIN FRANKLIN

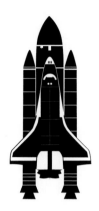

TEN

YOUR PERSONAL GROWTH VEHICLE

Unlimited ROI

MY FACE WAS ON FIRE as a mixture of recklessness and fear washed over me.

What have you done, you fool? Put your hand down!

The voice in my head was trying to talk some sense into me, and I don't remember a time when my arm felt that heavy. But I hushed the voice and shot my arm up even harder into the air.

It was the first day of a Tony Robbins event I'd paid $100,000 to attend. I had a question about an exercise we'd just completed.

But it was really a question that stemmed from my own present frustrations concerning my company—and it showed.

I knew from the moment Tony's gaze met mine and his giant frame barreled toward me that I was going to get the metaphorical stuffing kicked out of me.

My comment? Irrelevant.

My real problem? Apparently glaringly obvious.

I was about to be on the receiving end of one of Tony's classic hard-core interventions. I braced for impact.

Why am I so scared? Isn't this what I wanted?

Massive growth is hard in *any* form. I have willingly learned that lesson repeatedly in my life, and I voluntarily plan to keep learning it until the day I am no longer on this earth. Sadly, the reality is that most will never experience massive growth. I'm talking about the kind of growth that comes only through the guidance of an objective and highly qualified third party.

Over the next hour, my newest mentor, Tony Robbins, worked to get to the heart of my problem. My company was consistently growing—but at an agonizingly slow pace. I was discouraged but too deep to identify the issues myself.

It's pretty hard to see the label from inside your own box, right?

Then along came Tony. He peered deeply into my soul as only Tony can and saw what I had been missing. After the intervention was over, I experienced an incredible moment of victory. Thanks to Tony Robbins—the twentieth mentor I had hired and far from the last—I figured out how I was self-sabotaging my results.

I had to step out of my own way.

My first phone call after that much-needed verbal flogging changed my trajectory forever. I dialed the number of the most talented, qualified person in my organization, and I told him to print some new business cards. I was ready to relinquish management in my own company and name him CEO of my empire.

I credit that single decision with creating a 400 percent growth in revenue over the next year, growth made possible by choosing to invest in myself. I chose to spend six figures in the hopes that I'd experience an intervention just like the one I had. I needed someone to guide me past my own limitations, beliefs, and knowledge.

The following year, I doubled down and spent a quarter of a million dollars on mentorship with Tony. Not surprisingly, I once again saw incredible growth as a direct result of the mentorship. My company doubled again, and my profits quadrupled.

What had Tony told me that day that spurred such huge and profitable changes? I would share it all if I felt it would create value for you, but that lesson was for me and my specific challenges.

The point is that we all have blind spots. And all too often, we look to money, investment vehicles, and "hacks" to improve our life, when the truth is that our highest ROIs will always come from uncovering those blind spots and overcoming limiting beliefs.

I learned a powerful lesson from one of my mentors to whom I paid over $1M just to work with him. He taught me that the only dangerous information is *what we don't know*. Since then, I finally stopped arguing as if I knew best—because, in actuality, I only knew what I knew.

In fact, what you know can only get you more of what you have gotten in the past. You need proximity to people *far* more successful, genius, and experienced in what you are trying to grow if you want the fastest shortcut to the result.

The Power of Proximity

For over a decade, I have been paying the world's most successful people to provide me with the ultimate shortcuts to success. I've spent hundreds of thousands of dollars on mentoring (one mentorship came with a $1 million price tag that I'd gladly pay again). I'm talking about mentors who already possess 10 times the results I dream of and then some.

They are people who already arrived at "have it all," and now they're offering to share the map.

The people I choose to bring into my life reveal the potential I never even knew existed. They are the kinds of individuals who fill me with more than just "monetary fuel." They fill me with enough "rocket fuel" to blast me to the moon and back again!

We're talking about space shuttle-level results with unlimited ROI!

I've hired mentors to refine and improve the real estate and business philosophies I've painstakingly developed over the years.

- I've hired mentors to teach me how to cut body fat while increasing muscle mass.

- I've hired mentors to heal from growing pains in my marriage and scars from my childhood.

You name an area of personal or professional growth—I've hired someone to maximize my understanding in that area and find victory.

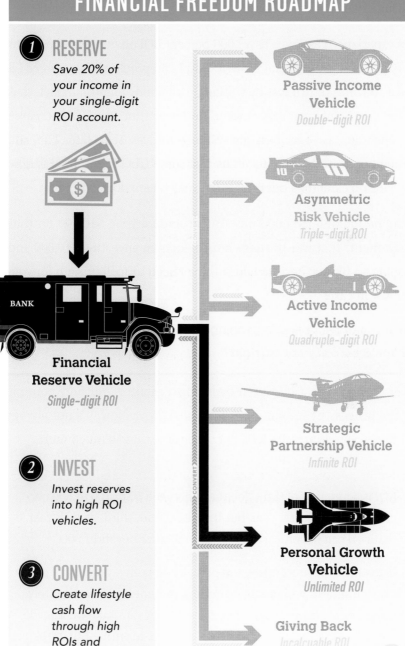

FINANCIAL FREEDOM ROADMAP

1 RESERVE
Save 20% of your income in your single-digit ROI account.

Passive Income Vehicle
Double-digit ROI

Asymmetric Risk Vehicle
Triple-digit ROI

Financial Reserve Vehicle
Single-digit ROI

Active Income Vehicle
Quadruple-digit ROI

2 INVEST
Invest reserves into high ROI vehicles.

Strategic Partnership Vehicle
Infinite ROI

Personal Growth Vehicle
Unlimited ROI

3 CONVERT
Create lifestyle cash flow through high ROIs and reinvest.

Giving Back
Incalcuable ROI
(Revealed in Chapter Eleven)

BANK

Milky Way-sized growth doesn't happen by chance. It happens by having a plan, executing that plan, and bringing in reinforcements.

I've experienced as much as a 1,000-percent ROI on money poured into personal and professional growth. And I can practically *guarantee* I'll see a 10-times return just by working with a new mentor. In fact, that is my bare minimum expectation. And over time, the ROI increases exponentially as your operating system improves. Years later, I am still benefiting from this mind shift as that same CEO I promoted is now working on extending our impact to over a billion dollars in value.

Imagine making a $1,000 investment and earning $10,000 on that investment. That is a 10-times return. Imagine investing $10,000 and reaping a $100,000 benefit. I don't think I need to spell this out for you, but just in case:

What if you could invest $100,000 and make $1M? Would you do it? You'd be crazy not to, right?

Every time I invest in myself by hiring a mentor and fully commit to the process by remaining teachable, I grow. Now, it's not always 10-times. Sometimes, it's less. But other times, it's so much more.

ROI is a function of time. You may only get a 50 or 100 or 500 percent ROI in the first year, but by the second, third, or fifth year, that ROI can become a ludicrous number far beyond 1,000.

Investing in your mindset and perception is always worth it and every upgrade will create a lifetime of benefit. Unfortunately, most people limit how much growth they can take in. They'll commit to growth by reading a book a month—but books just aren't enough. In my circles, people passionately commit to growth hacking by any means necessary. We move beyond books for good ideas and have graduated to having one or more mentors at any given moment and attend several masterminds and personal growth or mindset-related events a year.

You need to get in front of people who think far *beyond* the box and *beyond* conventional advice. You need a mentor who's been where you want to go and is still there! You need someone who can offer you the kind of perspective you could *never* have on your own.

If you've ever heard of Moses, you may be familiar with the story of the Israelites' exodus from Egypt. Imagine how overjoyed they were when Pharoah finally let them go after centuries of captivity. Suddenly, they went from being enslaved to becoming a freed people!

But then Pharoah changed his mind, and he sent his entire army after the Israelites in a blind rage. Unfortunately, the terrified Israelites soon reached a dead end in the form of the Red Sea.

At that point, they saw only two options. They could stand and fight and face certain death, or they could surrender and go back into captivity. But God had a third solution for them—*the Red Sea solution.*

None of us can truly understand how that moment must have felt for the Israelites. To suddenly see that water part and know that you are going to make it.

Am I comparing mentors to God? Absolutely not! All I want you to take from this amazing story is to try to imagine that feeling of *breakthrough.* There will be times when it feels like your business or your personal life are under attack from all sides, and there's nothing you can do but fight or surrender. But what if someone else from outside your perspective could help you find another way?

Wouldn't that person be worth their weight in gold?

No matter how stuck you feel or no matter how permanent a brick wall or closed door (or body of water) in your life may seem, my experience is that someone out there knows how to help you break *out* and *through*—and continue doing so for the rest of your life.

Grow every year, and after a few years, you won't even recognize yourself or your business. Growth on top of growth—the ROI is essentially incalculable on that type of progress. You are not only learning new skills and abilities from your mentors, but you are also expanding the perception of possibility and teaching your mind that you can truly have it all.

At the time of writing this book, I am working on three different businesses with billion+ dollar potential in the next five years, and that is all the result of constantly growing by working with mentors and implementing their insight.

Books are good for the beach, and they're a good way to have some quality quiet time in the morning, but books won't get you where you need to be if your goals are audacious and outrageous and worthy like mine.

Your brain is like a computer. But a computer is only as good as its programming. Are you running on a sleek MacBook Pro, or do you still use a clunky IBM desktop? If you want better, faster results, you need a software upgrade.

And when your computer requires an upgrade, what should you do? Should you read a book on how to upgrade the software or take it in to see a specialist who knows how to make it happen?

The path to lightning-fast results is not littered with books and online courses. Books and online courses are important, and I'm an avid consumer of both. But they are not sufficient *substitutes* for working one-on-one with mentors, nor do they provide the same 10-times and beyond growth.

The fastest way to achieve immense growth is to get into the airspace of human beings who have *already* achieved tremendous growth. Tony Robbins calls this principle "The Power of Proximity."

> **THE POWER OF PROXIMITY (NOUN):**
> The force and influence of other people's experiences and wisdom that you can harness by putting yourself in the physical vicinity of people who have already accomplished what you want to achieve.

It turns out I had been living this principle for 10 years before I knew it had an actual name.

- Want to double your income?

- Want to start a business with minimal time commitment?

- Want to invest in real estate with a high probability of double-digit ROIs?

- Want to learn how to pick moonshots?

- Want to let go of the past traumas that you allow to hold you back?

- Want to take your core relationships to new heights?

Everything you want—someone else already knows how to get it.

Unfortunately, the Power of Proximity also works the other way. We become the average of the five people with whom we spend the most time. That realization often makes people do a *hard swallow* as they think about their inner circle's limited mindsets. Here is a quick comparison:

Add together the approximate annual incomes of the five people with whom you spend the most time. Divide the total by five. That number will more than likely predict your income, plus or minus 10 percent. Here's an example:

David	$37,000
Martha	$51,000
Jesse	$44,000
Wyatt	$62,000
Porter	$40,000
Your income:	**$46,800**

Now imagine spending time with five people who make high six figures or more a year. Do the same math to determine what your income would be in that scenario. Here's an example:

Mickey	$1,200,000
Teresa	$600,000
Jimmy	$1,500,000
Jennifer	$450,000
Will	$800,000
Your income:	**$910,000**

Which income is more appealing?

The beliefs about money of those around you will rub off, one way or another. They will hold you back or rocket you toward financial freedom.

My net worth grows every year thanks to the Power of Proximity. I only spend time with growth-minded, highly driven mentors with big goals and even bigger plans for execution. I credit mentorship as the single most crucial investment decision I make.

It's truly the *ultimate* growth hack.

Coaches vs. Mentors

There is one word that has taken over social media and just won't stop. That word? *Coaching.* Everyone and their great aunt have become a coach. It's crazy! I've never seen anything like it.

As you may notice, I intentionally avoid the use of that word in this chapter. The reason is that you don't need a coach. *You need a mentor.* Many people think the two terms are synonyms, but I respectfully disagree.

The reason goes back once again to the Power of Proximity.

Coaches are great a being cheerleaders and encouragers! They may also be qualified to explain techniques, answer questions, and help get some results. However, at some point, it's likely that coaches have stepped outside the actual game. So, they can drill the perspective, but they are doing it from the outside looking in.

Mentors have mastered the results you seek and have created 10-times or better results—and they are also still actively in the game. Mentors are the best of the best. They give you something to aspire to, not stories of the good ol' days when they were once the high school quarterback. They have more experience than their students and are therefore worthy of being admired and emulated.

The wealth mentors you want are already massively wealthy. The health mentors you want are presently strong and well. The connection mentors you want have thriving current relationships.

Mentors are experiencing the things you want *now*, not way back *then*. This is because they have not allowed rejection to stop them from reaching their goals. They also know to help others shake the shackles of rejection. Let's further examine why mentors are the superior choice with a side-by-side comparison.

ATTRIBUTE	COACHES	MENTORS
Success Level Reached	May have never even played the game professionally	Attained the highest levels of success and are still excelling
Current Success Status	Used to be the best, but the "glory days" are gone	Still the best at what they do
Views on Rejection	Held back by the fear of rejection	Have never allowed rejection to stop them from reaching their goals
Methods Used	Give drills and run plays to force students to invest blood, sweat, and tears	Have the ability to use their own success path as a shortcut for students
Perspective	An outsider looking in	An insider offering their students a way in
Motivation Techniques	Cheerleaders and taskmasters	Mindset and activity hackers

The distinction between the two is vital, and you have to ask yourself whether you want to learn from a coach or a mentor. In reality, there is rarely an appropriate scenario where I would ever choose to work with someone who considers themselves to be a coach.

For faster results, look for mentors, not coaches. They're qualified by their *tangible results*, not their mere *access to information*.

Find a mentor who has 10 times the results you're looking for—and if they're willing to work with you and it's a logical fit for you both, make the investment. They could be the key to your personal growth.

The Clichés Aren't Wrong

If you are ready to apply some 10-times power to your life, relationships, and business, your SWAN account holds the answers. That means it's time for another investment—not in property, not in a business, but in yourself. Or like one of my mentors Dolf De Roos says, it's time to invest in "the real estate between your ears."

When people begin this journey, the impulse seems to be to purchase investments first with their reserve vehicle. I'm not saying that is a bad strategy, but if you have to choose between a market or real estate investment and a mentor who can help you access superior opportunities with a superior mindset, I encourage my students to invest in mindset first.

But how much to invest? I can't make that decision for you. Only you can determine the actual percentage based on how many areas of your life require some objective feedback and insight as well as how big and aggressive your goals are.

The more "behind" you feel in the game and the faster you want to go, the more you should invest in mentors—because they accelerate results way beyond the limits of pure capital investments.

Mentorship undoubtedly leads to monetary growth. Since this has been a book about money (as I told you it would be from the beginning), I feel compelled to say that. However, the ultimate purpose of life is not to accumulate money. Societal constructs—what we are told to envy, who we idolize—make it *seem* like that, but it's not true.

All the money in the world can't fill the void of an otherwise empty life. *I've met plenty of miserable rich people.*

What you prioritize eventually rules your life. If you live for being a gym rat and disciplining your body, that's commendable. It's also easy to fall into the trap of valuing physical looks above all else. If you live to grow your bank account, you can set yourself up for a lavish retirement. But what if you get to retirement and your pursuit of money has left you with no sincere relationships? Who wants to retire completely alone? That sounds bittersweet to me (and far more *bitter* than *sweet*).

Self-worth should not be connected to net worth, body fat percentage, belongings, or friendships. Self-worth also requires its own kind of fuel—one that can't come from a SWAN account, a firm body, or a luxury car.

You need "rocket fuel" for your mind in the form of powerful mentorships.

There is a bigger picture to consider that goes beyond financials. I'm talking about getting an ROI on prioritizing your growth as a human being—and a parent, professional, son or daughter, spouse or partner, and friend.

We are multidimensional human beings. Everything we do in life falls into the category of money, health, relationships, or personal empowerment. Actively pursue growth in each of these areas for maximum fulfillment.

You're here to grow. And the fastest way to grow is to work with someone who pushes you far outside of your comfort zones. This is a significant part of the journey toward having it all. We all grow at different paces for so many different reasons, but a general guideline that *anyone can follow to maximize fulfillment is this:*

1. *Set intention and pick your path.* Pick your most aggressive form of growth that will help you reach a desired level or goal (such as books, courses, coaching, and mentors).

2. *Step outside of your comfort zone.* A good mentor stretches you far beyond what's comfortable. Everything you want, but don't yet have, is found outside of your comfort zone. You *must* get there, and it's hard on your own— but not for a mentor).

3. *Execute with accountability.* Once you have the plan in place and see the path before you, it's time for action. Remain teachable in order to maximize the results of whatever growth path you have chosen.

4. *Expect and track results.* Track your progress in every area of growth and never forget that ROI is the ultimate tool to gauge how effective any investment is—whether it be a personal growth or financial investment.

People *without* money always think the grass is greener on the other side. In some ways, it is. But is finding the greenest pasture or having the most zeros possible on your bank account statement really the purpose of life? Not to me.

Material possessions are *terrible* substitutes for actual substance.

True fulfillment cannot come from monetary gain. Making money is necessary to reach your goals but should not be the goal itself. Here is an example:

> *If you had the means to spend $50,000 on a once-in-a-lifetime vacation, would that trip itself be the end goal? I hope not. Think about what it took for you to earn the means to take such an extravagant trip. You earned that trip because the good choices you made enabled you to afford the luxury. That is the real victory here. Your wise decisions and intelligent execution led to the fulfillment of your dreams.*

We've all heard clichés about stopping to smell the roses and there being no dress rehearsals in life. But as annoying as clichés can be—they're always accurate, aren't they?

So, as we continue, commit to discovering how many more clichés you can bring to life. Because why not? You should dance like nobody's watching, laugh more (since it's the best medicine), run through that open door after another one closes, and be the change you wish to see in the world. After all, you only live once.

Clichés like these get a bad rap, but I make it a point *not* to ignore the wisdom passed down through the ages. When you ask people on their deathbed what they cherished the most in their lives, not one of them will say their bank account. *Never forget that.*

There really are no dress rehearsals. This is your one shot at doing it right, so why not make it count?

A Grand Design for You to Have It All

So, what is this book really all about then?

On the outside, it is the perfect tried-and-true formula for how to become a self-made millionaire (many times over). But as you now look more deeply, you begin to understand that more money equates to more options—options to make more time for better health; for deeper, more meaningful relationships; and for producing the means to create value and solve problems for people. In other words, beyond achievement, this book is really about fulfillment.

Fulfillment can't be bought. It can only come through the choices you make.

This leads us to the Grand Design of how to balance fulfillment in all three areas of life. The deepest fulfillment in life comes through personal growth, which is why it's the final piece in the *Have It All* blueprint. To further explain life's interconnectivity, I created a diagram to explain how these three life areas work together like a symphony:

1. *Wealth.* Financial freedom gives you the capacity to create value for yourself, your loved ones, and the world. Your wealth can generate fulfillment for others when you apply it correctly.

2. *Health.* Health is your strength, energy, and ability. It's total wellness, inside and out. Wealth without health is empty.

3. *Connection.* We are connected not only to those around us but also to ourselves. There is a link with our fellow humans that transcends what we think we know about the human body, mind, and soul.

Take a look at the diagram to further explore how the three areas intersect in The Grand Design to Have It All.

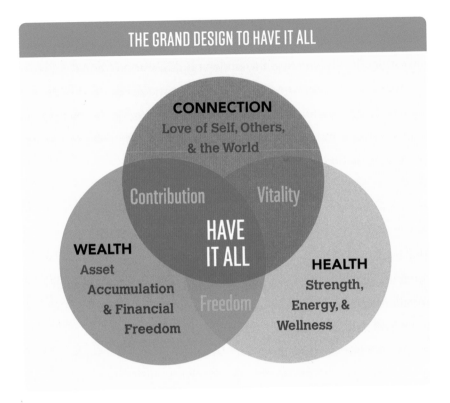

Where each of the spheres intersects, a new benefit develops. You could call these the "compounding ROIs" of having more than one area of life in balance:

- *Freedom* (the intersection of *health* and *wealth*). When you combine these two forces, you create extraordinary freedom. You have the energy and vitality to enjoy life to its fullest, and you have the financial resources to support anything you want to do.

- *Vitality* (the intersection of *connection* and *health*). The combination of these two forces is powerful! When you have your health, you feel energized to forge even more relationships. This produces a kind of vitality that allows you to experience life in all its vibrancy arm-in-arm with others.

- **Contribution** (the intersection of *wealth* and *connection*). When you combine money and connection, it leads to contribution. Being connected to the world enables you to see where your money would create the most impact. As you grow more financially stable, always look for how you can give back to the world.

And, of course, when all spheres are aligned, you have it all! Just remember that this is not a set "destination" you reach. Nourishing all three spheres requires conscious effort and a tireless commitment to foster each one, as well as ongoing mentoring.

Sphere 1: Wealth

The national average salary is $44,000 a year. I'm not sure what your life goals are, but I can almost guarantee $44,000 a year won't get you there. Set a reasonable income goal for the next year and then take the most critical step to find a mentor who makes far more than that and start working with them.

If a mentor doesn't tell you how much they make, find someone else. (I know, it's *so* taboo to talk about how much money we make, but, frankly, I think that's just another social construct we've created that needs to be eliminated.) Find someone you respect who can clearly explain how they achieved their financial freedom and then mirror their actions.

Wealth Mentorship

When I became interested in the real estate game, I aligned myself with immensely successful mentors who made tens of millions in the real estate game. I followed them, learned from them, and remained in their airspace as much as they would allow me to.

My first mentor eventually kicked me to the curb (a kick that I definitely deserved). I was a 22-year-old kid, desperate for help. I showed up at his house one night at 10 p.m. in a moment of excessive eagerness. *Please don't do this.* My second mentor expertly guided me through my first property investment. The equity from that deal led to 25 more homes over the next four years. My third mentor showed me the ropes of seller financing. He and I eventually partnered together on many real estate deals.

I've had numerous mentors in the real estate and financial arenas. To find the right wealth mentors, start defining what "next-level" wealth means to you. Dig deeply by asking yourself questions like:

- What would have to happen to achieve this level of wealth?

- Can my current job get me to this income goal? Why or why not?

- Does my mindset about money help or hurt this goal?

- What daily schedule changes would I have to make?

- Can I commit to saving at least 20 cents of every dollar I make?

Every time I wanted to learn something new that would accelerate my wealth accumulation, I skipped "Google University" and went straight to the experts. I'd determine who I could pay to get into their airspace and provide me with shortcuts to where I wanted to go.

Sphere 2: Health

Our health is our most incredible wealth. If life is a physical struggle, it's nearly impossible to find joy in the day. A healthy, strong body—one whose health is built from the inside out—is essential. Studies show there is a direct correlation between health and a person's income. That says a lot.

Health Mentorship

Almost a decade ago, I decided to enter a bodybuilding competition. I knew this meant I needed to figure out the best ways to trim the fat and get ultra-sculpted. The pressure was on—in a few short months, I'd be on a stage, half-naked, flexing in front of 1,000 people. My confidence was instantly boosted, knowing that my mentor had won multiple all-natural bodybuilding competitions. He assured me I could do it, and it was his confidence and success that got me there.

There are many areas of health for which you may consider hiring a mentor. You could hire a mentor who can help you cut fat and build muscle. You could hire a breakthrough coach to help you figure out the real emotions and meaning behind your health challenges. You could work with a mentor who can teach you how to eat well. You could hire a functional medicine professional who understands the most direct path to inside-out healing. Start defining what "next-level" health means to you by asking questions like:

- What would have to happen to achieve this level of health?

- Does my current lifestyle encourage or discourage physical wellness?

- Does my current mindset about my body help or hurt my goals?

- What daily schedule changes would I have to make to prioritize my health?

- Can I commit to making my health a priority every day by exercising, eating well, and getting enough sleep?

Whatever results you are looking for, find someone with a proven track record of transformative results and ask plenty of questions to ensure they are the right fit for you. Remember, they may have gotten to where you want to be and beyond, but they still need to prove it to win your trust and a share of your wealth reserves.

Sphere 3: Connection

We often stifle even the best relationships through our own self-imposed limitations ingrained in us from a young age. Childhood is riddled with limiting beliefs and traumatic experiences that we never outgrow. To make matters worse, unresolved issues from past relationships can manifest in other relationships. And unless you can move beyond the pain, your relationships run the risk of remaining unfulfilling and potentially toxic. It's certainly no way to live.

Connection Mentorship

Kalenn and I met when we were such young pups. As we worked to become better humans together, we discovered that what we thought was "good communication" wasn't always *good*. And it definitely didn't feel like *communication*. Finding the right relationship mentors was a game-changer for us! We learned communication techniques and were finally able to see each other through a more objective lens.

We even learned how to gamify our relationship's growth (I highly recommend this)!

Because of the improvements we experienced as a team, we are now relationship mentors for other couples. So, it's time to start defining what "next-level" connection means to you. Dig deeply by asking yourself questions like:

- What would have to happen to achieve an enhanced level of connection to others?

- Does my current lifestyle encourage or discourage genuine connection?

- Does my current mindset about relationships help or hurt my connection goals?

- What changes would I have to make to prioritize connecting with others?

- Can I commit to make my own needs (and the needs of others) a priority by actively working past the pain of former traumas?

Our relationships with friends, family, co-workers, and even the most casual acquaintances have a profound impact on heart, soul, and body. Learn how to foster and grow an unselfish devotion for others, and don't forget to cultivate some self-love while you're at it. You can't love others well until you first love yourself well (another cliché that is so true).

The Grand Design is awe-inspiring. What's even more impressive is that all facets of life fit into one of these three spheres. The goal, then, is to understand how to foster all three without neglecting any one area. A stool won't stand without all three of its legs. Likewise, your life will not function well when you neglect one or more of these spheres.

When you break down this book to one of its most fundamental truths, it is this: *your reserve vehicle needs to be a top priority.* Otherwise, how can you fund all of the massive growth you wish to experience in your wealth, health, and connections? The more money you have in your life insurance savings account, the more you have to pour into your investment vehicles and personal growth.

There will always be haters out there. People will tell you your dreams are crazy and foolish, or at the very least unattainable.

The thing is, they're not *always* wrong.

> Big goals *are* crazy if you have absolutely no clue how to accomplish them and no plan for figuring that out. We overestimate what we can do in a year and grossly underestimate what can be achieved in a decade. Add a massive personal growth component to your investment strategy and, within a decade, you will be blown away by what is possible.

This means the key is to not just stop at setting a goal. You need a plan! Your goals are *commendable* (*not* crazy) as long as you're willing to invest in a mentor who has 10 times the results that your growth demands.

As you seek to set your income and savings goals throughout this process, ask yourself questions like these:

1. How much did I make last year?

2. How much would I like to make next year?

3. What is the most I've ever made in a single year?

4. What's the most I've ever had in savings?

5. How much would I like to have in savings?

6. How much would I like to invest within a year?

It's essential to know the difference between how much you've made and how much you want to make. Working the numbers is the only way you'll ever be able to manifest the steps required to meet those goals. But you don't have to do it alone. The right mentor can help you come up with those steps.

Beyond the financial returns, the most significant ROI that you'll always get will be from an investment in yourself.

The day you start investing in yourself is the day you start opening up the real returns on your potential and discover what's possible in this life.

If you have made it this far in the book, it tells me you appreciate *my* ideas. That is a promising sign that you're a great candidate for achieving a life-changing experience at one of my live events, where you'll receive actual mentorship (and believe me—it's 10 times more impactful).

When you put yourself into my airspace for a few days, it will accelerate your growth timeline. You will experience the "next level" results you desire in wealth, health, and connections.

- Many of my students regularly double their income within months or a year of leaving my events.

- They feel empowered to start investing in real estate and moonshots (even those with no investment experience whatsoever).

To learn more about my life-changing live events, check out KrisKrohn.com/Experience.

Just two chapters left!

Are you going to stick with me to the end?

If so, I gotta say I like your style.

There has to be a reason I'd include the last two chapters in this book (because I'm not a "filler" kind of guy). So, I encourage you to read them. I'd be honored to speak with you at one of my events, and you can tell me about your experiences with this material and any feedback you may have.

My goal is to empower you to have it all. I hope I've achieved that.

CHAPTER TEN CHECKPOINT

1. Employ the Power of Proximity by getting into the airspace of mentors who have at least 10 times the level of success you aspire to achieve.

2. You need the "rocket fuel" that mentors can provide to create the kind of results you can't get from averaging the results of those in your inner circle.

3. If you have the choice between hiring a coach and a mentor, pick a mentor every time. They are walking, breathing success stories that you want to emulate.

4. Prioritize self-improvement through mentorship because all the money in the world can't fill the void of an empty life.

5. The diagram of The Grand Design to Have It All strives to bring the three spheres—wealth, health, and connection—into balance by actively nurturing all three.

6. The two paths to having it all have the same goal. Whether you are an employee with a thriving side business or a full-fledged entrepreneur, you must start stashing cash now!

We make a living
by what we get.
We make a life
by what we give.

WINSTON S. CHURCHILL

ELEVEN

YOUR BEST INVESTMENT

Giving Back

WHEN THE PANDEMIC HIT our world, every country around the globe reacted differently. Pakistan's approach was to enact a country-wide shutdown, which meant that all its workers were sent home. Essentially, no one was allowed to earn a living.

Many of the already-impoverished people there rapidly ran out of food. They no longer had the resources to take care of the basic necessities of life. I'm not exaggerating when I say that people were literally starving and dying in the streets.

One man whose family felt the total weight of the crisis was Murad, his wife Resham, and their toddler daughter, Roya. While goodwill volunteers were distributing food in the slums of Pakistan, Murad approached them and asked, "Do you want to buy my daughter for $710? She is two-and-a-half years old."

Surprised and, frankly, a bit shocked, they told him no. Murad then turned to his little girl and shouted, "You are a curse on us! From the time you were born, we are suffering. I wish you would have died the day your mother gave birth to you."

Precious little Roya started crying as her father screamed, unable to understand why her daddy seemed so angry with her.

The volunteers asked Murad why he was saying these things and why he wanted to sell his daughter (and for such a specific sum). He told them that he needed the money to pay for the freedom of Roya's mother, Resham. She was taken by their landlord after the family fell behind in their rent during 2020 when Murad was unable to work. The amount, $710, was three months' worth of rent.

The landlord had given Murad just one week to obtain the funds. Otherwise, he would sell Murad's wife to a brothel to repay the debt. During the wait, the landlord held Resham hostage in chains. It's painful to even imagine the horror Resham must have felt, and the corresponding despair, grief, and anger felt by her husband.

Murad told them, "I wish I could sell myself, but no one wants me. To save my wife, I have to sacrifice our only daughter."

Murad's plan was to sell his little girl into the sex trade for enough to cover his debts. Lose his wife or lose his daughter. It was a no-win situation for this man and his family.

When Kalenn and I found out about their desperate circumstances, we didn't hesitate. For us and so many other Americans and others worldwide, $710 is not a sum that we would miss.

On the final day of her captivity before Resham was to be sold, the missionaries we were working with showed up at the front door of the landlord's home to pay for her release. The young mother was in shock—she had no idea that she was about to be set free and would be able to hug her husband again and hold her little girl in her arms. She had braced for the worst but soon realized that she would soon be reunited with her loved ones. My wife and I weren't there to witness that moment, but we have no doubt it was something to behold.

For less than $2,000, we changed the course of a family's life forever (we also decided to pay for an additional three months of rent pre-payment to give Murad time to start working again). That is *a lot* of good for *very little* money in the scheme of things. That little family will never know who we are or even where the funds came from—and that doesn't matter to me in the slightest. I don't give for the sake of recognition. I don't give to "pay it forward."

I give because I literally feel *called* to give back. In fact, it's my most significant and most decisive calling in life and the real reason I created the Financial Freedom Roadmap.

While I have continued to increase my income year after year, our lifestyle has not changed one bit over the last decade. However, because of the financial freedom roadmap laid out in this book, we're making more money than ever. Years ago, we reached a point where all of our needs were met, and we lived a comfortable life. If my kids needed something, we could buy it without hesitation.

So, the question for my wife and I became, "Why pursue more? Don't we have enough?"

And the answer was, "Yes, we do have enough."

So, our mission then became to earn more to *give* more—and inspire others to give as well!

It's Time to Earn Your Wings

Our life's drive has become making an impact that matters. One of the most beautiful parts of becoming wealthy is that you have the opportunity to transition from being more *selfish* to more *selfless*.

True fulfillment comes when you move from the selfish life to the selfless life.

In a *selfish* life, you only make enough money for your own financial needs and wants. A *selfless* life happens when you follow these financial freedom rules long enough to produce more money than your own needs require. You then have the means to impact other people. Instead of all your financial goals and aims being self-centered, you reach a point where there's so much money that the purpose of playing the game is now about other people.

That is when you shift into *legacy thinking*.

When you are dead and gone, and your name is forgotten, what footprint will be left on this planet? Legacy thinking isn't concerned with making sure your family name lives on or ensuring that your name is on a plaque somewhere. It's about impacting people, not just while you are alive but also long after you are gone.

Impacting others and changing lives is what the final step in the roadmap is all about.

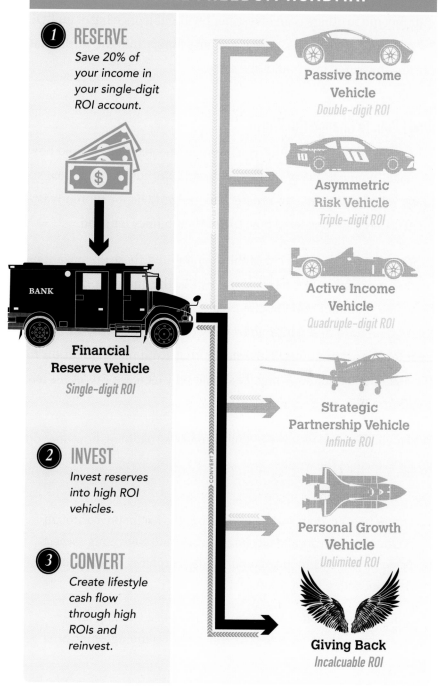

FINANCIAL FREEDOM ROADMAP

1 RESERVE
Save 20% of your income in your single-digit ROI account.

Financial Reserve Vehicle
Single-digit ROI

2 INVEST
Invest reserves into high ROI vehicles.

3 CONVERT
Create lifestyle cash flow through high ROIs and reinvest.

BANK

CONVERT

CONVERT

Passive Income Vehicle
Double-digit ROI

Asymmetric Risk Vehicle
Triple-digit ROI

Active Income Vehicle
Quadruple-digit ROI

Strategic Partnership Vehicle
Infinite ROI

Personal Growth Vehicle
Unlimited ROI

Giving Back
Incalcuable ROI

The angel wings on the roadmap represent the final and most critical investment—giving to charity. Giving away 10 percent or more of your income to others is an investment without a price tag or an ROI. It's genuinely priceless because it's an investment into the world that can't be measured in a traditional sense.

How I Plan to Change the World

When you study the wealthy, you'll notice they have discovered how to make the most out of their wealth. And not just through investment vehicles they use to create impressive ROIs for more investments. They have mastered how to use their money for good.

When the wealthy set up charitable foundations, those organizations represent a conduit for changing the world. The purpose of a foundation is so that after you die, the executor of your trust can keep the foundation alive and continue to grow it through healthy ROIs and additional contributions. This means that from one generation to the next, the foundation's impact should only increase. So, let me ask you this:

When you become wealthy by following this roadmap, how are you going to change the world?

I know how I'm doing it. My foundation, The Krohn Breakthrough Foundation, invests liberally into creating and cultivating a *whole person*—and this requires a particular emphasis on emotional freedom and self-empowerment.

The foundation offers emotional intelligence training and certified breakthrough work to those experiencing emotional distress. We teach people how to break free from their past, create a better future, and discover their purpose. Our mission:

We heal the brokenhearted by bringing breakthrough and emotional intelligence to the world.

I hold emotional intelligence at a higher status than academic knowledge. Lack of emotional intelligence is the primary culprit that keeps people from making good choices. In fact, behind every poor choice with a negative consequence is simply a limiting belief or a misunderstanding based on a lack of emotional intelligence.

When we created the Krohn Breakthrough Foundation, I knew we had crafted something extraordinary. We've been blessed to work with individuals from all walks of life, and we actively strive to partner with teachers across the country. Our certification program trains educators to help children overcome limiting beliefs that hurt them or lead to low self-esteem.

This allows kids to just be *kids*—to better experience the joys of childhood and build self-esteem. We endeavor to instill in the next generation the confidence to tackle life's peaks and valleys.

Our foundation also has a special heart for rehabilitating young women who have experienced the horrifying evils of human trafficking. We work to help them emotionally release their haunting memories and ultimately find peace, happiness, and healing. You can find out more about what we do and how we help by visiting our website:

KrohnBreakthrough.org

Our foundation also seeks to find the sick, the afflicted, and the hungry—those with real, palpable, gut-wrenching problems like Murad and his wife and daughter. We feed and clothe those who are in need.

That's the mission that we feel called to follow, and the conduit that made all this possible is also what fueled this book you now hold in your hands.

So, why am I telling you this? Why have I held nothing back in giving you the most successful financial roadmap? Can you imagine the impact it would have if those who read this book and implement the plan build the kind of wealth that enables them to give abundantly to the people, causes, and organizations who need it most?

Because this is the mission that empowers me to indeed have it all. Having it all means you have become the most generous giver that you can possibly be.

I also feel called to help others find a *why* for giving back that makes each gift more meaningful and fulfilling. One of my mentors, Robert G. Allen, taught me that the famous "pay it forward" idea is actually twisted. The belief that we should give in the hopes that "karma" or "the universe" will remember us on its way back around is really backward. Here is the truth that fosters a genuine giving spirit:

We give because we have already been paid in full!

Don't give to get. Don't give to create karma. Those are lovely ideas on the surface. However, what motivates someone who truly has it all is legacy thinking—and no, it's not about people remembering your name or even what you did. It's about people *feeling* the impact of your contributions for generations, whether or not they ever know how you helped them.

Give with a servant's attitude, and it keeps you humble. It also saves you from giving for any self-serving reasons. Some studies have shown that truly "altruistic giving" (wholly unselfish giving with no desire for recognition or reward) doesn't exist. I respectfully disagree. Give to give and for no other reason than people need you. They need me.

We need each other.

Give because you've already been paid in full! This is how we express gratitude for everything that we've received.

Ready for Breakthrough?

This is not a token chapter.

This is not fluff.

So, first and foremost, kudos to you for recognizing that a whole person is more than his or her bank account. Passionate human beings who contribute to their fellow man care about emotional intelligence as much as they care about financial intelligence (both are important).

I have found many meaningful ways to give back through the years. I've given back in the form of mission work and financial support for organizations, nonprofits, and my own foundation. I have also poured an untold amount of time and resources into my children's lives and the lives of other young people. I am also blessed to have the means to provide my parents with the ability to retire in peace.

Many people believe that the time for being philanthropic only comes *after* you're rich. But that's simply not true. The truth is:

The person you become in the process of building wealth is the person you will be once you have it.

Don't have money to give? Yes, you do! In today's world, a small amount of money has the power to have a meaningful impact. People are starving on the other side of the world where $0.30 buys a meal. And don't forget that you have time and talents to offer that can actually be even more meaningful.

> Give *before* you are wealthy, and you will experience an enduring kind of fulfillment.
>
> Give *before* you are wealthy, because in so many ways, you are *already* rich.

Your heart pumps, your lungs take in oxygen, and your eyes and ears experience the things around you. In other words, you've already been blessed—so give in gratitude. And as you become wealthier, you will have more to give.

To date, the resources I have shared with others have created so many of my life's most precious memories. It all started with wanting to take care of my parents in retirement. For over 10 years, I have paid their bills, sent them on trips, and made sure they have the resources to live a beautiful life.

If you dream about being a generous giver, the time to make that happen is *now!* I've practiced this from the beginning, and it's one of the reasons I feel immensely connected with the world. It also makes me a better husband, father, entrepreneur, leader, and mentor.

In Chapter Ten, I said that the point of life isn't to find the greenest pasture. Instead, work to leverage the true power of money by using it to achieve something *greater* than yourself outside your own pasture.

No one has ever found lasting fulfillment in having more *stuff*. At the final curtain call, what will matter is not a return on a financial investment but the return you receive on investing in others' lives.

As Tony Robbins says, "The secret to living is giving." Suppose you seek to build wealth only for security, travel, and other indulgences. In that case, it makes all of your aims and achievements about *you*. Those who live for personal gain tend to be the most miserable human beings on the planet.

Wayne Dyer once said that that which means much to you in the spring of your life will hold little meaning in the fall of your life. A time will come when possessions hold less meaning, and relationships become paramount. You may already be there, or it may not happen until you are much farther along. But make no mistake—it will happen. You can avoid the sting of regret by investing in others during *all* stages of life.

Maybe you haven't created your wealth yet, and that's why you're reading this book. The fact that you are reading this right now (and didn't stop after the "how to make more money" chapters) tells me everything I need to know about you. You are destined to leave a lasting legacy in this world, and it starts by using the vehicles in this book to amass enough wealth to make a colossal, lasting impact. Just remember to give at *every single step* along the way to financial freedom, not only at the final destination.

For less than $2,000, we kept a family together. That is money well spent! We kept a family together for less than the cost of one family vacation. That money may mean little to me, but that investment meant *everything else in the scheme of what really matters*. Guys—that is something, and there are countless other opportunities like that one to give a little to make a life-changing impact.

If you'd like to Awaken Your Financial Genius so that you too can pour into the lives of others, don't wait. Start today. If you don't have the financial means, give your time, your skillsets, or even your sweat equity.

You will never, ever be sorry that you did.

Ever.

CHAPTER ELEVEN CHECKPOINT

1. The call to give back is my most powerful calling in life, and it is what compelled me to complete the roadmap to financial freedom in this book.

2. Giving to others is what earns your angel wings on this side of heaven. A life lived for others is a beautiful thing indeed.

3. Don't give because you want the universe to return the favor. Give because you have already been paid in full!

4. There is no reason to wait until you are wealthy to give. The person you become in the process of building your wealth is the person you will be after you have it.

5. The secret to having it all is not a secret. Live a selfless life, and you will feel and experience what it's like to live life to its fullest.

6. Donations of your money, time, and energy—no matter the size—can have a massive, lifelong impact. When you give with the right motivation, you will change the world!

What do
you want, Mary?
Do you want the moon?
If you want it, I'll throw a
lasso around it and pull it
down for you. Hey. That's a
pretty good idea. I'll give
you the moon, Mary.

GEORGE BAILEY

TWELVE

IT'S A WONDERFUL LIFE:

Financial Freedom in Five Years

IF YOU'RE LIKE ME, Christmastime isn't Christmastime until you've watched *It's a Wonderful Life*.

The 1946 classic is about George Bailey—a salt-of-the-earth kind of guy with big dreams but an even greater sense of justice and devotion. It seemed George's purpose in life was to rescue his friends, family, and neighbors. He saved his little brother from drowning, his dad's business from collapsing, his childhood boss from prison, and his entire town of Bedford Falls from becoming victims of old man Potter's greedy schemes.

He had plans to travel the world and make his mark. Yet, George found himself stuck in Bedford Falls, running the family business after his father passed. His brother? A decorated war hero. His best friend? An ultra-wealthy jetsetter. Then, there was George—hometown dud (in his eyes anyway) after all of his greatest dreams were thwarted by his own good deeds. But he did manage to fall in love with Mary despite his cynicism. Together, they built a life with their four children.

He had his entire path all mapped out, and he wanted to give Mary anything she wished for, too. If she wanted the moon, he'd lasso it for her.

I dreamed of finding a girl worth lassoing the moon for—and one day, I met her. I knew almost from the beginning that Kalenn was the woman I wanted to spend the rest of my life with. I also knew I would do everything in my power to give her whatever she wanted.

One of my favorite parts of falling in love was the hours we spent dreaming about the life we wished to create. One of our priorities from the start was to provide our children with a world-class education—not through textbooks but through seeing and experiencing the world firsthand.

My financial freedom blueprint paved the way for that and so much more. To date, our family has visited 40 different countries. We hired a professor from a prestigious university to be our children's private educator. We also have two additional private educators, as well as multiple subject matter experts that help educate our children.

I have taken each of my four children on solo trips with me. We built beautiful memories visiting incredible places and some of the most pristine nature destinations. My oldest daughter and I even hiked the Inca trail and saw the beauty of Machu Picchu together.

Kalenn and I took our children to Kenya on a service mission to help build an orphanage, provide a way for the villagers to get electricity, and create clean water solutions. I want my kids to live their lives fully aware of how different their reality is from most other people. They live a privileged existence that the majority of the world could never fathom. And no matter your net worth, I can say the same thing about your kids if you live in the United States of America.

To experience the beauty, emotion, and fragility of this life side-by-side with my children—I can't put a price tag on that. I'm thankful for the memories my lifestyle has enabled me to create. I also remain in a profound state of gratitude, knowing I don't have to think about my bank account.

- If my kids need something, and I believe it's good for them, I buy it.

- If someone needs my time, and I feel called to give it, I provide it.

- If a solution necessitates money, and I feel inspired, I just need to know where to send it.

I *know* I have it all, and I want to make sure I never lose sight of that as George Bailey did. I don't want an Angel second-class named Clarence Odbody to have to come down from heaven to remind me how wonderful life is.

I want to live in a way that proves I *already* understand.

It took me years to design the roadmap in this book. I didn't have any shortcuts, and the path to having it all wasn't laid out before me. **Fortunately, you now have that path.** I had to make hard choices every day, and those choices are what brought us here together.

You are reading this because:

1. *I chose* not to fit a square peg (society's broken game plan) in a round hole (my life). Instead, I determined to find a better way to take control of my financial destiny.

2. *I chose* to pour savings not into my wife's 401(k) but into a life insurance savings account that we controlled.

3. *I chose* to invest money into property and build a real estate empire.

4. *I chose* to find a way to use the power of market risk to my advantage.

5. *I chose* to start my own businesses—thriving businesses requiring little time but retaining rewarding profit margins.

6. *I chose* to leverage my prior successes to access others' resources and form mutually beneficial strategic partnerships.

7. *I chose* to be a life-long student—to remain willing to invest in myself, be teachable, and stay hungry for the next lesson from my mentors.

I fueled my bigger dreams to produce even more incredible rewards by unleashing the full power of my five steps to financial freedom. I have now chosen to share that roadmap because everyone deserves the chance to have it all.

So now, it's the moment of truth ...

Do you believe you are destined to follow the traditional wealth path? Go to college, get a job, clock in and out, buy a house, pay it off, stash cash in a 401K, retire, and then greatly diminish your lifestyle, so you don't run out of money before you die?

That is the path most of your friends are on right now. But now you have the roadmap to financial freedom! So, what are you going to do with it?

When you start utilizing **single-digit ROIs** with a life insurance savings account, you will undoubtedly be better off than you would have been.

When you unleash the power of **double-digit ROIs** in real estate, you'll be able to retire with enough wealth to feel unrestricted a decade or more down the road.

When you master the **triple-digit ROIs** possible with asymmetric risk investing, you will achieve your wealth accumulation goals in years rather than decades.

When you unlock the master sequence and discover the power of **quadruple-digit ROIs**, you truncate that timeline even more—from years to possibly months.

When you step into **infinite ROIs**, there are truly no more limits. It's no longer a question of if or how but how fast.

When you add to all of this the **unlimited ROIs** you can experience through the power of proximity and mentoring, there will be no stopping you. And if you've focused on living a *selfless life* through it all, you now have the means to change the lives of countless others and make the kind of impact others only ever dream of making.

All of the resources the wealthy use to get wealthier—you've got them. So now, I'm going to tell you something that I wanted to say to you from page one, but I needed to earn your trust first.

> If you follow the plan to initiate this formula,
> true financial freedom can be completely available
> to you in less than five years.

It's not luck. It's math. ROI is the magical equation that allows you to compare opportunities and make the absolute best financial choices.

It goes back to the flywheel principle. The more strategies from this book you consistently implement, the more rapidly you will experience a financial breakthrough. Before long, you'll be shattering your previous financial ceilings and racing toward new heights you never thought possible.

Is it possible in five years or less? Absolutely! **You want the moon? It's yours to lasso.** Just follow the roadmap:

1. *Set up your reserve.* Set up your financial reserve through a life insurance savings account. It's free, and, more importantly, it's an intelligent way to fuel up your investments. **Visit KrisKrohn.com/CashFlow** for a free consultation.

2. *Learn how to buy real estate.* To get started in the real estate game, visit **KrisKrohn.com/Invest** to request a private call with one of my specialists. They will review your current financial situation and explore the possibilities for creating a passive income through real estate investing.

3. *Explore the advantages of asymmetric risk.* To take advantage of my research on emerging industries and exciting high-ROI companies, check out **KrisKrohn.com/Stocks**. Let me teach you how to leverage risk in the stock market to experience triple-digit ROIs.

4. *Discover a thriving business.* If you're interested in starting a thriving business or side hustle, go to **KrisKrohn.com/Thrive**. One of my team members will explore active income options to help you transition from your current job. And if you love your career, you can discuss ways to supplement your income.

5. *Develop partnerships that unlock infinite ROI.* Once you start following the Financial Freedom Roadmap, believe me when I say that it won't be hard to find people who want to partner with you. Your momentum will be contagious! Go to **KrisKrohn.com/Mavericks** to download your free copy of the resource I created to guide you through the process of developing a team of investor partners.

6. *Gain proximity to experts.* If you are interested in gaining proximity with me, visit **KrisKrohn.com/Experience** to unlock a special Have It All discount on my next live event.

7. *Never stop learning.* If you enjoyed this book, you may enjoy my other books, including *The Conscious Creator, Limitless,* and *The Strait Path to Real Estate Wealth.* Learn more by visiting:

> **Web: KrisKrohn.com**
> **YouTube Channel: Kris Krohn**
> **Podcast: "Have It All" with Kris Krohn**

George Bailey felt as though life dealt him a lousy hand. He was stuck in a drafty old house with a broken banister, trapped in the family business, and saw no way to escape his sleepy little town.

And yet, even though none of those facts ever *changed*, George went from wanting to end his own life to overflowing with gratitude by the film's conclusion. He accomplished this by undergoing one thing:

George Bailey went from miserable to grateful because of a simple perspective shift.

Life depends entirely on perspective. If you try hard enough to be miserable, you can always find more "broken banisters" and less joy.

George was wallowing in self-pity. He was about to be destroyed by one of old man Potter's schemes, and he was ready to end his life to escape the torment of it all. That is until his quirky but caring angel Clarence showed George how his friends and family would have been negatively affected without him.

George Bailey had it all—but he didn't know it until he almost gave it all away.

At the end of *It's a Wonderful Life*, Clarence (who finally got his wings) told his new friend George Bailey that "no man is a failure who has friends." George was the "richest man in town," not because of material wealth. It was because of the wealth in his heart he had accumulated by helping others.

I invite you to see how wonderful life is in the present moment. Before you add one more dollar to your bottom line, you are already blessed beyond measure. Take that attitude with you as you follow my blueprint, and I can almost *guarantee* the fulfillment you seek.

God made you for a particular purpose that is unique to you alone. And while I may not know you personally, I believe that your desire to live an extraordinary life is just as important as my desire for the same. My prayer is that this book gives you the insights you need to guide you on the path to living a wonderful life and *having it all.*

Best wishes to you, my friend,

ENDNOTES

1 Ben Steverman, "Half of Older Americans Have Nothing in Retirement Savings," *Bloomberg*, March 26, 2019, https://www.bloomberg.com/news/articles/ 2019-03-26/almost-half-of-older-americans-have-zero-in-retirement-savings.

2 Emmie Martin, "Here's How Much Americans Have Saved for Retirement," *CNBC*, June 26, 2019, https://www.cnbc.com/2019/06/26/how-much-americans-have- saved-for-retirement.html.

3 Teresa Ghilarducci, "Americans Do Not Have Enough Retirement Savings, Really," *Forbes*, March 28, 2019, https://www.forbes.com/sites/teresaghilarducci/2019/03/28/ no-americans-really-do-not-have-enough-retirement-savings/?sh=1692504b2b21.

4 Margi Murphy, "Scientists Claim Many People Could Soon Live beyond 120 Years Old," *New York Post*, June 29, 2017, https://nypost.com/2017/06/29/ scientists-claim-many-people-could-soon-live-beyond-120-years-old/.

5 Emmie Martin, "Here's How Much Americans Have Saved for Retirement," *CNBC*, June 26, 2019, https://www.cnbc.com/2019/06/26/how-much- americans-have-saved-for-retirement.html.

6 "Fast Facts," Employee Benefit Research Institute, 2020, https://www.ebri.org/retirement/publications.

7 Adela Suliman, "82 Percent of the Wealth Generated Last Year 'Went to the Richest 1 Percent of the Global Population'," *Time*, January 21, 2018, https://time.com/5111971/billionaires-global-inequality-income-oxfam-wealth/.

8 Burton Gordon Malkiel, *A Random Walk down Wall Street: the Time-Tested Strategy for Successful Investing*, (New York: W.W. Norton & Company, 2020).

9   John Schmoll, "What Is The Average Rate Of Return On A 401(k)?" *Investment Zen*, June 3, 2020, https://www.investmentzen.com/blog/average-401k-return/.

10   Associated Press, "Fidelity: Put Aside 8 Times Your Salary Before You Retire," *CNBC*, December 2, 2012, https://www.cnbc.com/id/49031856.

11   Annie Nova, "Why the 401(k) Won't Fix the U.S. Retirement Crisis," *CNBC*, February 14, 2021, https://www.cnbc.com/2021/02/14/why-401k-wont-fix-us-retirement-crisis.html.

12   "New Report: 40% of Older Americans Rely Solely on Social Security for Retirement Income," *NIRS Online*, January 13, 2020, https://www.nirsonline.org/2020/01/new-report-40-of-older-americans-rely-solely-on-social-security-for-retirement-income/#:~:text=A%20plurality%20of%20older%20Americans,as%20from%20defined%20contribution%20plans.

13   "How many American workers participate in workplace retirement plans?" *Pension Rights Center*, July 15, 2019, http://www.pensionrights.org/publications/statistic/how-many-american-workers-participate-workplace-retirement-plans.

14   Taylor Tepper, "Studies Confirm That Half Of Americans Struggle With Retirement," *Forbes*, October 6, 2020, https://www.forbes.com/sites/advisor/2020/10/06/studies-confirm-that-half-of-americans-struggle-with-retirement/?sh=5e8aa5c26f9f.

15   Kathleen Elkins, "Here's the Age at Which You'll Earn the Most in Your Career," *CNBC*, November 2, 2018, https://www.cnbc.com/2018/11/02/the-age-at-which-youll-earn-the-most-money-in-your-career.html.

16   "Retirement Security: A Compendium of Findings About U.S. Workers | October 2020 Supplemental Survey," *TransAmerica Center for Retirement Studies*, December 18, 2020, https://transamericacenter.org/retirement-research/20th-annual-retirement-survey.

17   Sabrina Speianu, "March 2020 Monthly Housing Market Trends Report: A First Glimpse of COVID-19 Impact on the U.S. Housing Market," realtor.com, April 2, 2020, https://www.realtor.com/research/march-2020-data/.

18   Jessica Dickler, "Most Americans Live Paycheck to Paycheck," *CNBC*, August 24, 2017, https://www.cnbc.com/2017/08/24/most-americans-live-paycheck-to-paycheck.html.

19   Kathleen Elkins, "Here's How Much Americans Have Saved for Retirement at Different Ages," CNBC, January 23, 2020, https://www.cnbc.com/2020/01/23/heres-how-much-americans-have-saved-for-retirement-at-different-ages.html.

20   Cameron Huddleston, "More Than 47% of Americans Aren't Investing Their Money," *Yahoo! Finance*, July 22, 2019, https://finance.yahoo.com/news/more-40-americans-aren-t-090000530.html.

MEET KRIS KROHN

Kris Krohn is a bestselling author, speaker, breakthrough mentor, real estate guru, and expert wealth coach. For well over a decade, Kris has mentored thousands of people in creating, managing, protecting, and growing wealth through innovative real estate investing and other key strategies. Kris also empowers people to grow their wealth, health, and personal power through high-ROI investments and his powerful Limitless Belief Breakthrough. He helps people bridge the gap between where they are and the results they want in every aspect of their lives. Sharing his knowledge has become Kris's life passion and purpose.

Kris's other books include *The Strait Path to Real Estate Wealth*, *The Conscious Creator*, and *Limitless: Reclaim Your Power, Unleash Your Potential, Transform Your Life*. With his books, platform, video trainings, live events, and nonprofit (Krohn Breakthrough Foundation), Kris lives to teach people the mindset behind creating the life they want. Kris regularly puts on live experiences to spread his message of transformation and financial liberation to the world. Learn more at **www.KrisKrohn.com**. Kris holds a bachelor's degree in marriage, family, and human development from Brigham Young University and an honorary MBA from Stevens-Henagar. He and his wife, Kalenn, are the proud parents of four beautiful children.

NEXT STEPS
Where Do You Go From Here?

You've now been inundated with a lifetime's worth of information, tips, tricks, and eye-opening financial and wealth accumulation truths that may leave you wondering where to go from here.

I'd like to make things a little simpler and remove some of the guess-work. Simply visit the link below for access to ALL of the free resources, tools, and next-steps guides discussed throughout this book:

KRISKROHN.COM/HAVEITALL

If you are looking for breakthrough, I also recommend finding out more about my multi-day live events. I'd also love to connect with you on social media, so reach out to me on any or all of the platforms!

KRISKROHN.COM
Instagram: *@kriskrohn*
TikTok: *@kriskrohn*
Twitter: *@kriskrohnREI*

Facebook: *@MentorwithKris*
YouTube Channel: *Kris Krohn*
Podcast: *Have It All*
LinkedIn: *@MentorwithKris*

NOTES

NOTES

NOTES

NOTES

NOTES

NOTES

NOTES

NOTES

NOTES

NOTES

NOTES

NOTES

NOTES

NOTES

NOTES

NOTES

NOTES